TURKEY

PROFILES · NATIONS OF THE CONTEMPORARY MIDDLE EAST
Bernard Reich and David E. Long, Series Editors

Turkey: Coping with Crisis, George S. Harris
Israel: Land of Tradition and Conflict, Bernard Reich
The Republic of Lebanon: Nation in Jeopardy, David C. Gordon
Jordan: Crossroads of Middle Eastern Events, Peter Gubser
South Yemen: A Marxist Republic in Arabia, Robert W. Stookey
Syria: Modern State in an Ancient Land, John F. Devlin
The Sudan: Unity and Diversity in a Multicultural State,
John Obert Voll and Sarah Potts Voll
Libya: Qadhafi and the Green Revolution, Lillian Harris
Bahrain: The Modernization of Autocracy, Fred Lawson
The United Arab Emirates, Malcolm C. Peck
North Yemen, Manfred W. Wenner
Iran, John W. Limbert
Algeria, John Entelis
Afghanistan, Ralph H. Magnus
Oman, Calvin Allen
Tunisia, Kenneth Perkins

Also of Interest

*The New Arab Social Order: A Study of the Social Impact of Oil
Wealth*, Saad Eddin Ibrahim
OPEC: Twenty Years and Beyond, edited by Ragaei W. El Mallakh
Economic Growth and Development in Jordan, Michael P. Mazur
The United Arab Emirates: Unity in Fragmentation,
Ali Mohammed Khalifa
Libya: The Experience of Oil, J. A. Allan
Food, Development, and Politics in the Middle East,
Marvin G. Weinbaum
Israel's Nuclear Arsenal, Peter Pry

About the Book and Author

This comprehensive survey of the Turkish experience traces the Turks through the ages to provide the background essential to understanding contemporary Turkey. Noting the problems that possession of an empire left for its modern successor state and evaluating the role of the military in Turkish politics, Dr. Harris provides insight into the political challenges facing the country today and finds that the success of policies for economic development is the key to overall political success in modern Turkey. He analyzes the most recent constitutional structure, showing how modifications in proportional representation have helped create a more effective government. Turkey's position in international politics remains anchored to the United States and the West, he states, although recent efforts to broaden economic ties with the Middle East have been quite successful. In addition, the Cyprus issue continues to powerfully affect Turkey's larger alliance relationships. Dr. Harris concludes that Turkey has the resources and the dedication to representative government necessary to solve its most pressing problems.

Dr. George S. Harris is director of analysis for the Near East and South Asia in the Bureau of Intelligence and Research, Department of State, Washington, D.C., and has been a lecturer at Johns Hopkins University. Among his many publications are *The Origins of Communism in Turkey* and *Troubled Alliance: Turkish-American Problems in Historical Perspective, 1945–1971.*

To
the memory of
George Sellers Harris, Jr.

TURKEY
Coping with Crisis

George S. Harris

Westview Press • Boulder, Colorado

Croom Helm • London and Sydney

Profiles/Nations of the Contemporary Middle East

Photo credits: Nos. 2, 5, 6, 8, 9, 11, 12, 15, 16 by the author. Nos. 1, 3, 4, 7, 10, 13, 14, 17, 18, 19, 20, 21, 22, and 23 are courtesy of the Turkish General Directorate of Press and Information. Photos 24 and 25 are courtesy of the newspaper *Milliyet*. Photo 26 is courtesy of the United States Information Agency.

Copyright © 1985 by Westview Press, Inc.

Published in 1985 in the United States of America by Westview Press, Inc.; Frederick A. Praeger, Publisher; 5500 Central Avenue, Boulder, Colorado 80301

Library of Congress Cataloging In Publication Data
Harris, George S. (George Sellers), 1931–
   Turkey: coping with crisis.
   (Profiles: nations of the contemporary Middle East)
   Bibliography: p.
   Includes index.
   1. Turkey—Politics and government—1960–
I. Title. II. Series.
DR593.H37 1985   956.1′03   85-10645
ISBN 0-86531-239-7

Published in 1985 in Great Britain by Croom Helm Ltd., Provident House, Burrell Row, Beckenham, Kent BR3 1AT

British Library Cataloging in Publication Data
Harris, George S.
   Turkey: coping with crisis.—(Profiles: nations of the contemporary Middle East)
   1. Turkey
   I. Title
   956.1′038   DR417
ISBN 0-7099-3786-5

Printed and bound in the United States of America

10   9   8   7   6   5   4   3   2   1

Contents

Tables and Illustrations

Partial Key to Turkish Pronunciation

c = j as in jail
ç = ch as in church
g = g as in get
ğ = y, or lengthens the preceding vowel
ı = i as in sir
i = i as in inch
j = zh as in azure
ö = eu as in French deux
ş = sh as in shell
ü = ue as in French rue

A circumflex accent softens the preceding consonant.

Acknowledgments

Production of a book such as the present volume, which is a distillation of what I have learned about Turkey in more than thirty years of study, truly reflects the cooperation of many. Numerous friends and colleagues in Turkey and the United States have helped over the years to develop and enrich the ideas expressed in this work. I am especially indebted to the generosity of Professor Enver Ziya Karal, my mentor at Ankara University, whose untiring explanations of Atatürk's Turkey gave me unique insights into a bygone era. The opportunity to meet İsmet İnönü and to know a generation of leaders of the Republican Peoples party also informed the presentation that follows. University colleagues in Turkey, and in the United States as well, provided both a foil to test my notions and a font of useful suggestions and new interpretations on all phases of Turkish existence. As much of the following text concerns current happenings, journalists have also been of important assistance in contributing to my understanding. Beyond all those who were professionally involved in the events under analysis, I have benefited much from the opportunity to discuss anything and everything with good Turkish friends, whose feelings about their own society animate my conception of Turkey in all its dimensions.

Needless to say, none of those who have contributed in any way to my endeavors are responsible for my interpretations. They are my own personal observations; they do not necessarily represent the positions and policies of the U.S.

Department of State, which has been my employer for much of the recent past.

I cannot close without a word of heartfelt thanks to my long-suffering family. Their unfailing understanding and their quiet cooperation buoyed me up in what often seemed an unending task. My wife, Jo, in particular, has shown rare patience and forbearance during these most trying times.

George S. Harris

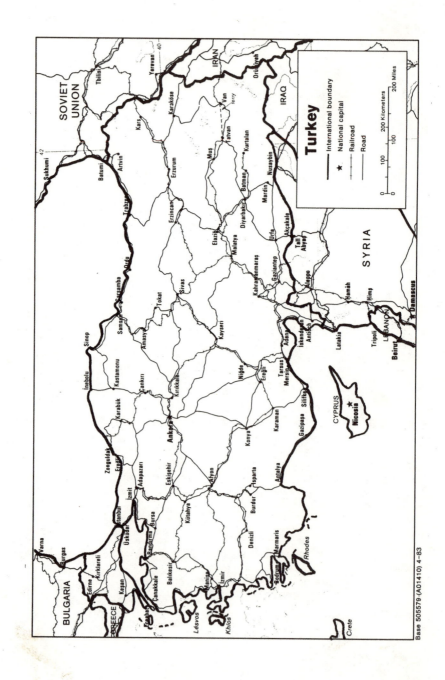

Turkey

- International boundary
- ★ National capital
- Railroad
- Road

0   100   200 Kilometers
0   100   200 Miles

SOVIET UNION

BULGARIA

GREECE

IRAN

IRAQ

SYRIA

LEBANON

CYPRUS
★ Nicosia

Varna
Burgas
Edirne
Kırklareli
Keşan
İstanbul
Üsküdar
Çanakkale
Bandırma
Bursa
Balıkesir
Manisa
İzmir
Lésvos
Khíos
Foçabaşı
Denizli
Marmaris
Bodrum
Rhodes
Crete
Kütahya
Eskişehir
Afyon
Burdur
Isparta
Antalya
Adapazarı
İzmit
Ereğli
Zonguldak
Karabük
Çankırı
Kastamonu
İnebolu
Sinop
Kırıkkale
Ankara
Konya
Karaman
Gazipaşa
Silifke
Mersin
Tarsus
Ereğli
Niğde
Kayseri
Amasya
Tokat
Samsun
Çarşamba
Ordu
Sivas
Trabzon
Artvin
Batumi
Sukhumi
Erzincan
Erzurum
Kars
Karaköse
Muş
Van
Taivan
Elazığ
Malatya
Diyarbakır
Batman
Kurtalan
Mardin
Nusaybin
Urfa
Akçakale
Gaziantep
Kahramanmaraş
Tall Abyaḑ
Aleppo
Hamah
Ḩimş
Latakia
Tripoli
Beirut
Damascus
İskenderun
Antioch
Adana
Tbilisi
Yerevan
Orūmīyeh
Sukhumi
Tatvan

40
42

SYRIA

Introduction

Turkey has become an increasingly popular subject of study in recent years. Its geographical position on the edge of Europe, the USSR, and the Middle East gives it a special significance. As one of the small number of non-Western societies struggling to evolve a workable parliamentary democracy, it has long seemed to offer lessons and insights into an important political process. At times, some even have regarded it as a model for other developing countries.

But the need to understand the Turkish experience has gained additional urgency in the past few years from the dramatically rising challenges to its democratic experiment. The smooth evolution of Turkey's political, social, and economic structure can no longer be taken for granted. Moreover, its geopolitical significance attracted renewed attention following the outbreak of the most acute stage of the Cyprus dispute with the Greek-speaking world in 1974. The resulting damage to Turkey's Western partnership raised serious questions about the country's orientation and the course of alliance politics, just at a time when economic disarray and political turmoil at home were becoming the order of the day. The military takeover of 1980 came when revolutionary disorder in Iran to the east and an upsurge of Islamic fundamentalism in various parts of the Muslim world were heightening interest in Turkey.

Not unnaturally, therefore, research has proliferated into many facets of Turkish existence. Since World War II, Western historians, followed by political and social scientists, have made ever more penetrating studies of Turkish reality. The literature on Turkey in Western languages is voluminous and growing.

The Turks themselves commenced somewhat later than their Western contemporaries in making major efforts to analyze their own society in depth. A generation ago, translations of the works of outside observers were the main fare produced in Turkey. Since the 1960s, however, a new crop of Turkish researchers has produced a flood of material on their own country. Many had political axes to grind. In order to design the appropriate Marxist strategy for development, for example, they focused on whether the country had passed through feudalism. This quest led from elite studies—which still capture attention among Western scholars—to investigations of such diverse phenomena as the organization of tribes in eastern Turkey and the political and social behavior of slum dwellers on the outskirts of the main urban centers.

The need to meet often acute economic crises since World War II imparted further impetus to Turks to inventory their society. Not only were increasingly sophisticated studies of the Turkish economic performance required by the international financial community, but the move toward centralized planning also demanded investigation of Turkey's economic and social development. As a result, demographers and economists have come into their own in the universities; their services were sought as advisers to government and the political parties. Burgeoning private industry also sponsored research into the Turkish economy.

Analysis of Turkish society has benefited from the increasingly frequent exchanges between Turks and their foreign counterparts. Major celebrations for the fiftieth anniversary of Turkey as a republic and for the centennial of the birth of Mustafa Kemal Atatürk, modern Turkey's founder, have stimulated new research. Other international gatherings of interdisciplinary experts have contributed to the diagnosis and prescription for Turkey's challenging problems.

Yet the answers remain elusive. Although the accretion of knowledge about Turkey over the decades since World War

II is striking, the important areas of continuing uncertainty are also impressive. To be sure, figures matter in Turkey. Relatively reliable statistics about numerous aspects of society do exist—something that cannot be said about many other developing polities. Nonetheless, despite this expanding data base, studies of Turkey have not progressed to the point where a "standard" view of the country and its prospects has emerged. Thus far, attempts to present Turkish reality as a coherent whole have been rapidly outdated; the polemical literature of recent years remains less than satisfying as well. Indeed, all too many major questions of historical controversy still have not been convincingly resolved.

Accordingly, to attempt a broad overview of Turkey is to sail in often uncharted waters. What follows, therefore, is not so much an assemblage of generally accepted assertions as an idiosyncratic effort to explain a complex society in rapid motion. Many scholars would not subscribe to all the propositions advanced below. Some of the analysis runs directly counter to theories that, up to now, have occasioned little challenge. But Turkish studies are not yet at the point where even fundamental matters can be accepted without further critical inspection.

The story of modern Turkey properly begins with an exposition of the land and the people. The physical and cultural geographies are so central to the Turkish equation that they are more often than not taken for granted and thus relegated to minor mention in all but the most specialized literature. Yet Turkey's politics—not to mention its social and political life—are powerfully influenced by regional and sectional as well as religious differences. Beyond the dichotomy of rural and urban life customarily acknowledged in recent literature lie various other divisions that play a role in such central Turkish concerns as violence and economic development. Despite the imprecision of data on the different population groups, it is thus important to identify them as completely as possible.

An understanding of the achievement of the modern Turks is possible only through an inspection of their historical antecedents. Some of the clues to the present lie buried deep in the past. Thus a survey of the traditions and evolution of the Turkish elite is particularly pertinent to an elucidation of the structure of politics in Turkey in more recent times. Such a review also permits an appreciation of the reasons underlying Turkey's present boundaries, ethnic composition, and even its basic foreign orientation.

Turkey's urgent requirements for foreign assistance have occasioned intensive study of the economy. The connection between economic matters and political life, however, is generally accorded secondary attention. Thus, while attempting to sketch out the broad lines of Turkey's economic progress and problems, the present work will focus on an explanation of the interrelationship of economic and political factors. Only on this basis is it possible to understand the economic dimension of democracy in Turkey.

An understanding of the environment in which the political game is played forms a necessary underpinning for an analysis of the institutions that give Turkey its particular political structure. Although the application of the new constitutional order elaborated during the latest period of military rule is still being worked out, the written precepts of the constitution have always had special relevance in Turkey, where legal forms have long conditioned political behavior. Given the newness of the present rules of the game, the system of parties is especially important in forming the backbone of the political structure. It is necessary to understand the intricacies of the voting system, which continue to affect the outcome of the political contest in subtle but significant ways. And it is important to recognize the continuity in political behavior from one constitutional period to another.

Obviously a key actor in Turkey's political order has been the military establishment—a special form of pressure group on the Turkish scene. The armed forces have played a prominent (and at times a determinant) role, even when not actually running the government. An investigation of the reasons underlying this military intervention is thus essential to an assessment of the long-term prognosis for civilian rule.

At the outset, it was suggested that foreign policy considerations played a part in attracting the attention of scholars to Turkey. But only in the past decade have Turkey's alliances and alignments been studied in any detail. Even this work, however, has not yet focused on an unraveling of the complex interaction of domestic and foreign policy. Thus it is especially important to relate these two complementary aspects of Turkish politics.

Despite the obvious difficulties in looking into the future, the present study will seek to draw conclusions about the evolution of current trends. Perforce highly speculative, this section will identify continuing problems and evaluate the likely success of the Turkish regime in handling these challenges.

1

The Land and the People

Turkey's geostrategic position, size, resource base, and population place it among the more important states of the world. Nonetheless, its relatively low level of economic development in comparison with the Western industrialized powers limits its scope of independent action. Indeed, in a number of social and economic respects, as well as in its geographical location, Turkey occupies a transitional position between Europe and the Third World.

Sharing a boundary with the Soviet Union on the northeast, Turkey also borders Iran, Iraq, Syria, Greece, and Bulgaria. It thus sits astride the land routes to the Middle East from Europe and European Russia. The outlet of the Black Sea into the Mediterranean, an increasingly busy sea-lane for Soviet commerce with the Middle East and Africa, flows through its territory.

This physical location at the junction of continents has profoundly influenced Turkey's political, social, and economic courses. After the losses of territory in the Balkans in the last days of the Ottoman Empire, the country was left with a European lodgment in Thrace constituting only slightly more than 3 percent of its national area. Yet Turkey's orientation for more than a century has been Western. At the same time, the 97 percent of the state located in the Anatolian peninsula of southwest Asia gives Turkey a Middle Eastern underlay that links it to its Ottoman past.

Among the larger states of the world in area (36th in rank order), Turkey is a land of pronounced contrasts in such matters as geographic features, climate, ethnic and religious

8

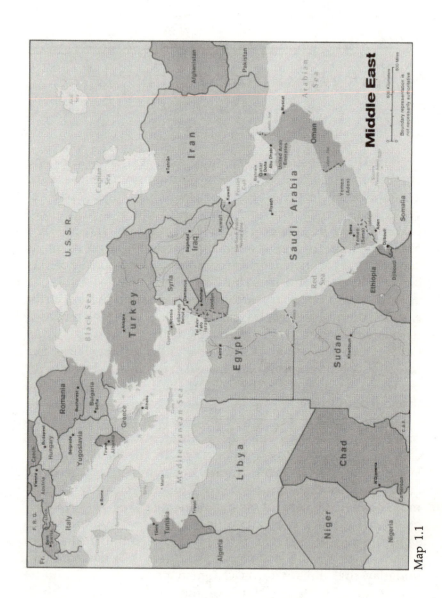

Map 1.1

composition, and regional economic development. Turkey's total area of 301,380 square miles (780,576 square kilometers) is over 40 percent larger than France. That figure includes the inland Lake Van and Tuz Golu as well as the Bosporus/ Sea of Marmara/Dardanelles outlet of the Black Sea.

GEOGRAPHIC VARIATION

For statistical purposes, the country is often divided internally into eight geographic regions: Thrace, Black Sea, Marmara and Aegean, Mediterranean, Western Anatolia, Cental Anatolia, Eastern Anatolia, and Southeastern Anatolia. These groupings of contiguous provinces also display more or less distinctive social, economic, and political complexions.

Thrace is an extension of the Balkan steppe of gently rolling terrain, separated from the rest of Turkey by the waterway that links the Black Sea and the Mediterranean. Its moderate rainfall and temperate climate make its land well suited for cereal farming. The rural population in these provinces is now increasing only slowly in size, despite the moderately high birthrate. This fact indicates that the lure of urban life is pulling many Turks off the farm. Villages near İstanbul, the former Ottoman capital and still Turkey's largest city, are profiting from this flow; many are rapidly burgeoning into bedroom communities for commuters to the country's commercial and manufacturing center. İstanbul's urban heart, however, slowed in its growth in the late 1970s in both absolute and relative terms as compared with previous census periods. Yet, with its cosmopolitan life-style and heterogeneous populace, the city of 2.77 million (according to the 1980 census) remains overall the most attractive destination for Turkey's increasingly mobile inhabitants.

The Black Sea provinces are among the most developed in Turkey. Rugged mountains hug the coast along almost the entire littoral. The steep hillsides, which have similar temperatures but far greater precipitation than does European Turkey, are suited for hazelnut and tea cultivation. Minerals abound in the mountains in the western part of this region. And Zonguldak, with its extensive coal reserves, is a center

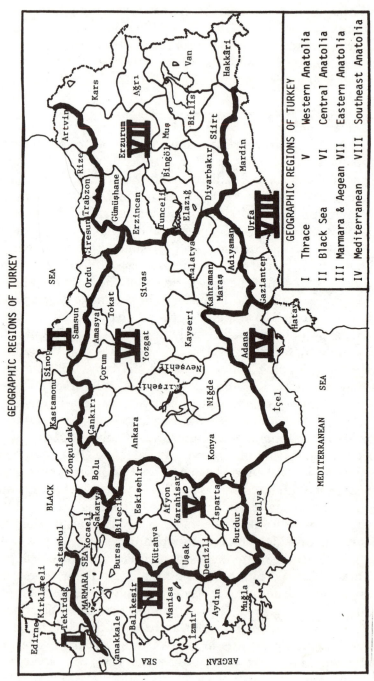

Map 1.2

for mining and the steel industry. The Laz, who are centered in the eastern portion of this region, are distinctive in accent from other Turks, but they have not shown ethnic solidarity in other ways.

The provinces bordering on the Sea of Marmara and the Aegean coast form a relatively urbanized, fast-growing area, including the major city of İzmir (population 758,000 in the 1980 census) and the Asiatic suburbs of İstanbul. This region, too, is a major agricultural area, where cotton is raised in the river valleys and fruit is cultivated on the hillsides. With dry summers and mild, rainy winters, agricultural yields on the fertile soils are good. These relatively developed provinces provide ready access to the Anatolian plateau to the east through gradually sloping mountains and easily traversed valleys. The economically active inhabitants of this area, some of whom are immigrants from the Balkans or the Crimea, traditionally formed the base of support for Turkey's center-right parties. In the Third Republic, this somewhat conservative political constituency has thus far been split between the free enterprise–oriented Motherland party and its right-of-center rivals, the Nationalist Democracy party and the True Path party.

Along the Mediterranean coast to the south, the littoral provinces with their semitropical coastal plain are cut off by steep mountains from the Anatolian highlands to the north. Hot, dry summers in this region are followed by wet, mild winters, which permit the cultivation of citrus fruit and bananas along the coast. Profiting from its climatic advantage over Western Europe and the Middle East, this area has also become Turkey's center for the production of early market vegetables for export. Like the Aegean coast, the Mediterranean littoral is growing rapidly in population. Thanks to its easy access to the outside world, it ranks high in terms of modernity in Turkish terms: its populace is consumer oriented and has had the highest level of consumer-durable purchases per capita in the country.

Western Anatolia stands as a transition zone from the coast to the dry, cool interior plateau, which occupies the major portion of the Asia Minor peninsula. These western provinces, with only secondary cities, are marked by generally slow population growth. Still basically agricultural in occupation, this is Turkey's center for the production of opium, a product that provides the maximum profit from marginal land even when sold legally at government-set prices. It is also an area of rug-weaving and textile production. A major battleground in the Struggle for Independence, its then underpopulated terrain received a major share of the Balkan immigrants in the population exchange of the 1920s. Additional immigrants have joined them in succeeding decades. These transplants from the Balkans, like their fellow immigrants in the neighboring Aegean provinces, have also been reliable supporters of right-of-center parties.

Central Anatolia forms an exception to the general trend toward decreasing modernity in moving from west to east and from the coasts to the interior. The statistics are skewed by the dominance of Ankara (population 1.88 million in the 1980 census), Turkey's second largest city and after İstanbul the most powerful magnet for migrants. These migrants come from the rural areas but also include the highly educated city dwellers in search of the professional opportunities offered by the bureaucracy. In contrast, other Central Anatolian cities, such as Konya and Sivas, which were important caravan stops in Ottoman days, have shown significantly less potential for growth. The central provinces are a major wheat-producing area. Given their dry, temperate climate, they also support fruit tree cultivation as well as sheep and cattle raising. Religious diversity characterizes this region: a major part of Turkey's Alevi (Shiite) population lives in Ankara and the provinces to the east; the mother convent of the Mevlevi (Whirling) dervishes is located in its western reaches; and the home base of the Bektashi dervishes, traditional rivals of the Mevlevis, lies in its central section. This diversity is echoed in the contrasting voting patterns of the various provinces of this region and in the volatility of its voters, whose party allegiance has proven relatively unstable.

The eastern Anatolian provinces bordering Soviet Russia, Iran, and Iraq are mountainous with thinly covered lava terrain. This region of sparse vegetation, with its short summers and severe climate, is generally suited for animal husbandry rather than settled farming. Industrialized only to a small extent, these provinces have the high birthrate and low contraceptive use associated with the prevalent religious conservatism of the population. A steady stream of migration from the northern portion of this region has resulted in population declines in some provinces in the latter 1970s. By contrast, the southern provinces have been among the most rapidly growing in Turkey. This southern area, where most of Turkey's 6 million or so Kurds are to be found, is distinguished by language and culture from the rest of Turkey. Banditry has been endemic in eastern Turkey; terrorism and separatist propaganda by Kurdish groups were among the important factors precipitating the military takeover in 1980.

Southeast Anatolia, comprising the provinces of Gaziantep, Mardin, and Urfa, represents an extension of the north Syrian plain. Home of the bulk of Turkey's some 600,000 Arabs as well as numerous Kurds, this region resembles Eastern Anatolia in its predominantly tribal social organization. Economically, it is also among the least developed parts of the country. The area, which is primarily agricultural, with hot, dry summers and mild, dry winters, supports sheep raising in the east and irrigated farming in the west. Lacking industry to absorb its excess labor, it has seen many of its more productive elements migrate to other parts of Turkey or even outside the country, leaving behind a very young population. At present, construction of the Atatürk dam, Turkey's largest hydrological project, is providing a temporary boost to employment in these provinces.

POPULATION TRENDS

The dynamism of Turkey's population is confirmed by the 1980 census. The 44,737,000 Turks recorded in that enumeration are increasing at a rate of just over 2 percent annually, down from the 2.5-percent growth recorded in the preceding period. That decline probably reflects the effects of increased urbanization, expanding contraceptive use, and a continuing flow abroad. Emigration, however, is slowing the rates of population increase achieved in the early 1970s, when European demand for labor was at its peak. The rates may also be declining as a result of improved health conditions, which are gradually reducing the pressure for the large family sizes of the past, when infant mortality was extremely high. Government propaganda to discourage population growth does not appear responsible for a significant portion of the decline in the rate of population increase; although the authorities favor the spread of birth control devices, the regime has not been particularly active in encouraging their use. Yet even in the rural areas, women have been eager to avoid regular pregnancies.

Decades of relatively fast population growth have given Turkey a young population. Those under age 20 form almost exactly half of the populace. Accordingly, the pressure on educational facilities continues to grow and the requirement for new job formation to absorb the entrants to the labor force is disproportionately large.

Turkey's population is also increasingly mobile. Like most developing countries, Turkey has seen a major exodus from the farms in the past three decades. Today, slightly under 55 percent of the populace lives in rural areas, as compared to about 76 percent thirty years earlier. The speed of this flow now appears to be tapering off somewhat, as economic conditions in the cities have become more difficult. There is evidence that more workers now than in the past are preferring to eke out a living on marginal farms rather than risking unemployment in the cities. And the success of major agricultural projects, as with the Atatürk dam, could provide additional jobs in the rural sector.

MAJOR MINORITIES

Even though Turkey is far more homogeneous in ethnic composition and economic characteristics than was its predecessor, the multinational Ottoman Empire, the people of the modern Turkish state are still diverse in important ways. Muslims constitute about 99 percent of Turkey's population. The Sunni version of Islam clearly predominates as an inheritance from Ottoman orthodoxy. But especially in central and northeast Anatolia, the heterodox Shiite interpretation finds many adherents. Although the census does not distinguish between these two major forms of Islam, therefore making an exact count impossible, knowledgeable observers estimate that Shiites number up to 25 percent of the total population.

Most of the Shiites of Turkey, generally called Alevis (but not to be confused with the Alawites of Syria), do not espouse the tenets of fundamentalist religious activism advocated by Khomeini's Iran. Rather, they predominantly favor a politically reformist approach, including a nondiscriminatory secular stance. As a result, the Alevis were strong supporters of the left-of-center stand of Atatürk's Republican Peoples party. Their allegiance to that party, even in its most unpopular days, was shaken only by a brief dalliance with the tiny left-leaning Turkish Unity party at the end of the 1960s. When this small organization, in which Alevi leaders were prominent, failed to gain the momentum necessary to challenge the larger parties effectively, the Shiites returned to their former affiliation. In the 1983 elections, the Alevi vote appears to have split between the Motherland party and the Populist party; many of those who voted for the Populists evidently transferred their support to the Social Democracy party in the 1984 municipal elections.

The more visible role of the Alevis in recent decades has brought them into sometimes violent confrontation with conservative Sunnis. The celebrated clash between left-oriented Shiites and fundamentalist Sunnis in Kahramanmaraş in December 1978 was the most spectacular instance of religious conflict in modern Turkey. The shock over the depth of this communal hostility precipitated the imposition of martial law in various rural and urban provinces. But continuing enmity between adherents of these two wings of Islam erupted periodically in killings of members of one religious group by members of the other in the shantytowns around the major cities during the descent into anarchy that preceded the military takeover of 1980.

Although the far stricter controls imposed since that time

have suppressed this sectarian conflict, the resumption of civilian political competition has already given evidence that religion will not be easy to extirpate from politics, despite the precautions mandated in the new constitutional regime. The small Prosperity (Refah) party, which was organized in the summer of 1983, won a few of the mayoral contests in the municipal elections, thanks to its strong links to the banned National Salvation party of the previous regime, an organization that had sought to exploit religious appeal. Former adherents of the National Salvation party also form a faction within the Motherland party. Given the continuing role of religion in political affairs in Turkey, therefore, Sunni-Shiite rivalry seems destined to provide something of an underlay to politics in the Third Republic much as it did in the immediate past.

Kurds make up the second largest minority in Turkey. Census data indicate that Kurdish speakers make up over 10 percent of the country's population. They are distinguishable from the majority primarily by their language, although most are Shafii Sunnis in rite as opposed to the predominantly Hanafi Sunni Turks. Speaking two separate dialects of an Indo-European tongue from the Persian language family, they are concentrated in the band of provinces running from Malatya to Hakkâri in the east, where they border the Kurdish districts of northern Iraq and northeastern Iran. Although most of Turkey's Kurds are rural and are organized in tribal formations, urbanized and more or less detribalized Kurds make up the bulk of the inhabitants of the city of Diyarbakır; increasing numbers of Kurdish migrants are also congregating in the squatter communities in and around İstanbul and Ankara.

Turkey's Kurdish tribes are no longer nomadic; rather, they lead a pastoral, transhumant life under their traditional chiefs. The latter are frequently also leaders of dervish orders (especially the Nakshibandi and Kadiri) or belong to conservative religious sects (such as the Nurcular movement to restate Islam in fundamentalist terms), to which Kurds seem particularly drawn. These self-reinforcing political and social distinctions serve to perpetuate an identity quite separate from that of the mass of the Turkish population. But, at the same time, they ensure the division of the various tribes and clans into sharply rival units nourishing ancient feuds over such matters as grazing rights and marriage partners. Thus overarching Kurdish nationalism has not been the dominant trend among Kurds in Turkey. The three revolts of Kurdish leaders in the 1920s and 1930s failed to unite the tribal entities. Some loyalists even fought alongside Ankara's troops in putting down these insurrections. Indeed, men of Kurdish origin have risen as high as chief of staff of the Turkish Armed Forces during the republican era. Although small, clandestine separatist groups roiled the eastern provinces in the late 1970s, their activities were tinged with banditry and social protest against traditional tribal leadership practices. But the majority of the Kurdish people appears to have remained outside this political violence. No charismatic political leadership has emerged; to this day, it is not even clear that most Kurds in Turkey actually desire more than a greater opportunity for cultural and economic advantages.

This is not to say that the Kurdish problem has been or will soon be eradicated. Kurdish bands, perhaps based in or seeking safehaven in Iraq, harassed Turkish security forces in the frontier provinces in the fall of 1984. And as long as Kurdish dissidents receive aid and encouragement from their ethnic brothers in Iran and Iraq, such disturbances can be expected to persist.

More generally, Kurdish ethnic distinctiveness is fed by cultural and economic grievances. The use of the Kurdish language in publications or in education is prohibited, although the spoken tongue continues to flourish. A persistent complaint of Kurds arises from the fact that eastern Turkey remains comparatively underdeveloped. That will remain true even though the major dam program on the Euphrates has spurred construction activity in this area and will provide considerable additional irrigated land. Kurdish students at universities in the western part of the country and at Erzurum have at times urged a faster rate of development for their native region. Some Kurdish elements backed the small, now defunct socialist parties that before 1980 took up the cry for greater economic opportunity for these provinces. The outlawed Turkish Communist party still seeks to play on lingering Kurdish economic grievances in its quest for recruits through propaganda broadcast into Turkey.

In the Kurdish areas, tribal leaders have used their social and religious status as bases of political power within the multiparty democratic system. As a result, they have dominated politics in southeastern Turkey. Confident of their supporters, they have bargained for top positions on the major party tickets or have shifted to minor parties or run as independents as they saw fit. Indeed, the Populist party and the Nationalist Democracy party achieved their greatest electoral successes in the 1983 elections in various Kurdish provinces by forming powerful local alignments; the Motherland party also scored well through the same mechanism in other provinces with a heavy Kurdish population. The price tribal chiefs have paid for freedom to represent their social and religious constituencies in this way is to eschew all overt appeals to ethnicity. In fact, past categoric prohibitions against exploiting Kurdish identity on a larger scale have been repeated or strengthened in the constitution and legal structure of the Third Republic. The prospect of increased limitations on ethnic expression may have played a part in inducing five provinces predominantly inhabited by Kurds in eastern Turkey to show the highest rejection rate of any areas of the country in the referendum on the 1982 constitution.

SOCIAL DIFFERENTIATION

Another major cleavage with significant political implications is the sharp rural-urban divide. In effect, there are still two quite distinct Turkeys, although great improvements in communications, especially the expansion of the road network and the spread of television, are providing the rural populace increasingly intimate acquaintanceship with the culture of the modern developed sector. Many of the villages lack most of the rudimentary accoutrements of modern life. Living conditions and social customs have changed only very slowly in the more remote villages. By contrast, rural settle-

19

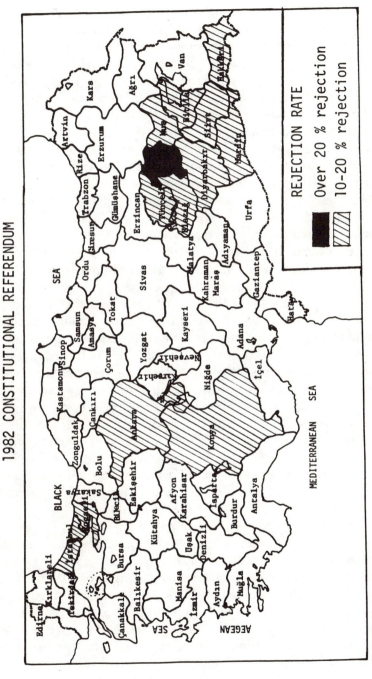

1982 CONSTITUTIONAL REFERENDUM

REJECTION RATE

Over 20 % rejection

10-20 % rejection

Map 1.3

ments in the vicinity of urban centers are rapidly becoming modernized in outlook and standard of living; many are becoming bedroom communities for workers in the larger cities. In between, there are villages that, in seeking to become part of the market economy, are opening themselves to pressures for modernization. Peasant insistence on better roads and more dependable supplies of clean water form the grist for political campaigns. Many of the peasants in the more developed regions have voted for parties that promise material improvements without challenging time-honored social patterns. And as peasants become exposed to city values, their willingness to follow the unquestioning dictates of their traditional leaders in voting for political candidates is eroding. Thus the circumstances under which the Republican Peoples party received 100 percent of the vote in the provinces of Hakkâri, Bitlis, and Siirt in eastern Turkey in the 1950 elections will almost certainly never be repeated.

Peasants moving off the farms have typically headed for İstanbul as their first choice. But rapidly growing squatter communities of rural migrants have come to surround all of Turkey's larger cities. Indeed, well over half of Ankara's population now consists of these transplanted villagers. Their sprawling mushroom housing, which usually groups people from the same geographic locality or region, represents a transitional stage between the traditional life of the village of origin and the modernized style of the city. Unemployment is high and living conditions relatively primitive in these ghettos as compared to standard city housing. But those migrants who do come see the city as offering more amenities and hope than the villages they have left.

The cities proper are the home of the elite and represent the modern, richer sector of the economy. They are the loci of education and literacy, for a population that is steadily gaining in both. City dwellers are strongly oriented toward the West in attitudes as well as in consumption patterns. They provide the national leadership for political parties, run the bureaucracy, and manage the economy. In short, they are the pacesetters of national life and culture, in that they establish the goals for the rest of society.

Turkish culture, for all the dynamic pressures on it imparted by continuing development and increasing mobility, remains highly status conscious. Age and position elicit respect among the elite as among the masses: the current party heads are all at least in their mid-50s, far older than new leaders normally brought to power by military interventions elsewhere in the world. Traditionally, government and military careers have been the most respected professions in Turkey, with education and the free professions ranking next. In recent years, however, business has increased in esteem, as the top ranks of industry have expanded and have come to command far better salaries and perquisites than those associated with the previously preferred careers. University education is more than ever the dividing line between the elite and the rest of the population. But the expanding numbers of educated urban dwellers are fragmented in political allegiance. The elite no longer proceeds in lockstep along a commonly agreed path as it did for the most part during Atatürk's era.

Unlike many of its neighbors, Turkey has brought its urban women into the mainstream of political, professional, and cultural life. The educational level among women is rising steadily, and women have not faced legal discrimination in their activities since the 1930s, when they were given the vote. Atatürk worked persistently to break the Islamic restrictions on women's activities outside the home. Although he achieved remarkable success in the urban setting, custom has maintained the traditional male-dominated pattern of life in the rural villages, where women are largely confined to household or agricultural tasks. As modernity penetrates the villages, however, even peasant women find their horizons expanded. Increasing numbers of rural women are migrating abroad to join their husbands and are entering the work force in their new countries of residence.

The government is the pacesetter in employing women. More than just token numbers of women serve as senior officials, and in the bureaucracy they are well accepted in positions of responsibility. The universities have also served as favorable environments in which women play important parts. They are widely represented in the free professions as well: some of Turkey's most prominent journalists, lawyers, doctors, and the like are women.

In political life, however, women have played a relatively small role. Politics is still predominantly a man's game. During the one-party era, Atatürk used parliament as a showcase of women's progress, ensuring the election of 16 handpicked women to the then 339-seat parliament in 1935. But with the advent of competitive politics, the ranks of female deputies thinned. Despite the active encouragement of women's organizations in all of the parties of the Second Republic, only 4 women won deputyships in the 450-place lower house in 1977. Of these, at least one was assured election by being named by her party national headquarters to a high position on the list from İstanbul. From this nadir, their numbers rose in the 1983 elections. At that time, 12 women were elected to the 400-seat parliament. Although some of these women had long-established family relationships with their party leaders, others had earned their positions without such advantages. In addition to winning seats in Ankara, İstanbul, and İzmir, women were elected in the considerably more rural İsparta, Edirne, and Ordu constituencies. In part, they benefited from the opportunities afforded by the removal of a whole established generation of politicians. But their success also testifies to the growing educational and professional level that women had attained in Turkey, for these candidates had already distinguished themselves in careers outside of politics. Yet even this improved showing does not suggest that women either will be strongly represented in future assemblies or will serve at top levels in political parties.

EDUCATION AND CULTURE

In recent decades, Turkey has made great strides in increasing the education and literacy of all its people. Since the early years of the republic, the state has seen control of education as one of the main ways to create a nation and unify the population. The task of schooling the Turks was not an easy one. Spread out in some 40,000 villages, this population required an enormous number of institutions and teachers. Starting in the urban communities, the republican administration embarked on imaginative efforts to create a nationwide network of primary schools. Next, village teacher-training institutions were set up in rural areas to keep the prospective teachers from becoming accustomed to the attractions of urban life. This experiment in teacher training, however, rapidly became a political issue between reformists and conservatives. After a generation of effort, these normal schools were shut in the 1950s. But the effort to open village schools continued, with growing success. And by the 1980s, some 50,000 primary schools, educating nearly 6 million students, were in operation. A quarter of these students went on to junior-high secondary schools, and half that number continued into senior-high institutions. In the past generation, the population of university students has risen some five times; by 1980, over 350,000 students were pursuing their studies at eighteen universities.

Although legal provisions instituted by the military rulers limiting the time youths can take to complete higher education have somewhat reduced those in student status, the number of serious full-time students has not been greatly affected. In line with the increasing emphasis on business, vocational and technical schools have tripled in number during the past two decades, while the number of students in primary schools has more than doubled. Turkey's literacy rate has also grown sharply, now standing at about 70 percent of the population over age 6 as opposed to about 40 percent in 1960. Illiteracy is highest in the southeast of Anatolia and lowest in the major cities. Illiteracy rates for women are still roughly double those for men, a proportion that has declined only slowly over the past generation.

Most students followed a secular academic curriculum. But starting in the 1960s, the government set up a religious training track for secondary students to prepare personnel for religious service. These schools grew steadily in popularity until the military takeover of 1980. Thereafter, the number of schools declined from just over 500 to less than 350 by 1981, and the number of students fell from over 148,000 to under 70,000 in the same period.

The rising educational level of the population underlies what has been one of Turkey's most pronounced and favorable trends: the impressive upward social mobility of its people. Education has been the main mechanism for moving into the national elite. Modest social origins have not been a bar to achieving high status. Although it remains quite unusual for national figures to celebrate their peasant origins as did Justice party leader Süleyman Demirel, few prominent politicians could equal Republican Peoples party chief Bülent Ecevit's pedigree from an elite family with links by marriage to the Egyptian royal house. Ecevit was again unusual in lacking a university degree, although he was clearly the most intellectual of the modern Turkish prime ministers. For the rest, the growing pool of educated people has given Turkey wide reserves of potential political leaders from which to draw, and it has undergirded the explosive expansion of international business activity by Turks in the past decade.

Republican Turkey has also paid considerable attention to developing the artistic potential of its citizens. The sultan's court sponsored painting and rug weaving in particular. Already in the nineteenth century, a few Turkish artists had been sent to Europe for training. They returned to give impetus to a transition from the art of the miniature, which had been most highly developed in Persia, to Western pictorial style. Perhaps out of respect for religious injunctions against re-producing the human figure, most Turkish artists of Abdül Hamid II's era concentrated on landscapes.

In the Young Turk period, European impressionists heav-ily influenced Turkish painters. Art in Turkey moved away from its rather stilted naturalism to a freer mode of expression. In subject matter and style, however, it was clear that these artists had completely turned their backs on the Islamic miniature tradition. Thus, by the start of the Turkish Republic, painting was shaped and influenced by Europe and not by Islamic models.

This emphasis on adapting and assimilating Western art gained even greater impetus in the republic. The leaders of modern Turkey were as committed to the West in art as they were in political and social life. They continued the tradition of sending their most promising artists of all mediums to Europe. This elite group staffed the Faculty of Fine Arts, which assumed the task of training a growing population of artists. Museums of painting and sculpture were also opened in the 1930s to house works, mostly by foreign artists. But in more recent decades, native Turkish painters have begun to satisfy the growing artistic appetite in Turkey.

Sculpture developed as a completely new art form in Turkey in the 1920s. Prior to that time, religious scruples had all but completely stifled that branch of endeavor. But Atatürk saw sculpture as an important vehicle to inspire patriotism in the Turkish population; as a result, the state since 1925 has commissioned large numbers of heroic statues. At first, it was necessary to rely on foreign sculptors. But by the 1930s, Turkish artists entered this field. And by the mid-1950s, Turkish sculptors were moving from figurative statues to abstract creations.

Architecture has had a long and honored tradition in Turkey. Islam required huge structures in which large congregations could assemble for Friday prayers. When the Ottoman treasury was relatively full, large buildings could be constructed. But in the more or less hand-to-mouth financial situation of republican Turkey, there were few major commissions. The building of Atatürk's mausoleum was entrusted to a gifted Turkish architect, and another famous Turk designed Ankara's main educational institutions. But in the absence of sufficient funding, architecture has rather languished in modern Turkey.

Music, on the other hand, has flourished. Turkish folk music, heavily indebted to a common source of inspiration in the Islamic neighboring states, has maintained a vigorous life. With its subtle repetitions on a limited tonal scale, it has been the mainstay of Turkish folk dancing, a form of entertainment that remains intensely popular. Turkish folk musicians on the *saz* (lute), *ney* (reed flute), violin, and bagpipe are widely honored throughout the land; from performances on radio and, now, on television, the names of the principal players are household words in Turkey. In the 1920s, the state began a systematic collection of Turkish folk melodies.

Tens of thousands of traditional tunes have been transcribed and recorded.

In addition to this thriving popular music, under the Turkish Republic the state has given special encouragement to finding and developing Western-style musicians and composers. A school for music teachers was opened in Ankara in 1924, and major Western composers were brought to Turkey to participate in organizing a State Conservatory of Music. These efforts have produced some well-known pianists and violinists. Turkish composers have also been active in producing chamber music and symphonies for Turkish performing groups and orchestras in the largest cities.

Complementing this musical activity has been a revival of Turkish folk dancing. Each region offers a distinctive type of folk dance. In some, the men and women perform separately; in others, mixed dances are also permitted. Certain dances portray stories of battles in heroic form. Others closely resemble the line dancing of the Balkans, for example, or the individual gymnastic-style displays of the Caucasus.

With strong Western support, Turkey has evolved a creditable form of ballet and opera. The Turkish state ballet company has established strong ties with prominent British artists who have supervised the training of successive generations of Turkish dancers. The State Conservatory graduated its first ballet students in 1957. Opera has a somewhat longer history in Turkey; the State Conservatory opened an opera department in 1938. The state has been the main patron of both opera and ballet. In İstanbul, the city government, as well, has sponsored a municipal opera since the early 1950s. But these major activities were within reach only of urban dwellers before the advent of nationwide television during the past decade. That, for the first time, has exposed the mass of the population at large to this essentially Western-style musical performance.

Theater has had deep roots in Turkey. Puppet theater may antedate the formation of the Ottoman state, and shadow plays (Karagöz, from the name of the hero) date at least to the seventeeth century. Western-style theater became popular during the reform period of the nineteenth century. It has had political overtones ever since. Some of Turkey's most radical writers, such as the famous Communist poet Nazım Hikmet, used this medium with effect. It was probably no accident that, among intellectuals rounded up for Communist sympathies over the years, actors and playwrights figured prominently. Although foreign works vie with native Turkish productions for a place on the Turkish stage, the language of these performances, as well as that in the operas, is almost always Turkish; hence these works are accessible to the urban population at large.

Finally, Turkish filmmaking has also grown in vigor since the first movie film was produced at the time of Turkey's entry into World War I. Growing originally out of theater performances, Turkey's cinematographic industry at first was mainly concerned with dramatization of plays. The development of movie techniques came slowly, however, as sufficient funds were difficult to secure for filmmaking. Financial limitations have continued to retard the evolution of the cinema industry. But a brisk demand for simple, cheap films skewed the industry away from quality productions. More recently, Turkish films have emerged as vehicles of social protest, leading the authorities in 1977 to set up a film censorship committee to prevent the importation or filming of material judged likely to damage national security or public morals. At least one underground film, *Yol* (Way), nontheless earned high acclaim in the West, although it was banned in Turkey. Moreover, the advent of the video cassette may make such tight national control difficult. Overall, filmmaking seems likely to come into its own as one of the most vigorous arts in Turkey.

Ağrı Dağı (Mount Ararat) in eastern Anatolia reaches 16,945 feet (5,165 meters) in altitude. In the Bible it is the legendary landing place of Noah's ark after the flood.

Bodrum, near the confluence of the Aegean and Mediterranean seas, is the Halicarnassus of the ancients, site of the tomb of Mausolus, one of the seven wonders of the world. Shown here is a medieval Crusaders' castle and the modern yacht harbor, now the scene of a thriving tourist charter trade in the summers.

The new city, Ankara, where many of the ministries are located. The tall building houses the Ankara branch of Turkey's largest department store chain.

Castle and surrounding slum housing district in Ankara. Many of these so-called *gece kondu* mushroom structures were originally built by squatters. Once the walls and roof were completed, the inhabitants could not be evicted. Now most have electricity and even TV sets.

Farmers' market in Ankara. Turkey's fruits and vegetables are especially tasty and many varieties are now shipped to Europe. Farmers dress in a rough adaptation of Western costumes or in even more distinctive peasant garb.

Threshing in Thrace by the traditional animal-drawn sledge. Mechanical threshing machines are also in wide use on the larger farms.

Villagers going to market on the traditional ox cart. This primitive transport is increasingly displaced by trucks and tractor-drawn vehicles.

Retail shops in Ayaş, near Ankara, in 1955. Urban sprawl has long since obliterated these establishments, but similar ones can still be found in the more remote areas of Turkey.

Greased wrestlers at a village wedding near Antalya on the Mediterranean coast. To celebrate such occasions, as a rule, there is lavish entertainment for the whole village.

Primary school teacher and class in an urban setting. Students at such institutions wear black smocks. The subject matter in this class is civics, an important effort to inculcate Atatürk's values.

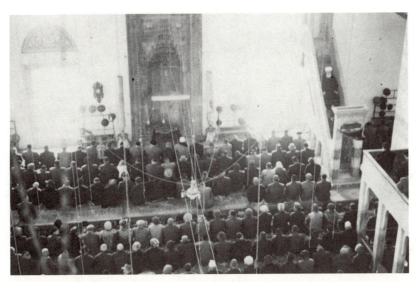

Worshippers in the mosque at Konya at Friday prayers. Men worship together on the ground level; women worship either in the balcony or off to the side segregated in alcoves. This mosque next to the tomb of the founder of the whirling dervishes is the gathering spot for some of Turkey's more conservative Muslims.

The Blue Mosque, Istanbul, one of the masterpieces of Ottoman architecture, was built in the early 17th century by Sultan Ahmet I. The small domes in the foreground belong to the religious school typically associated with a major mosque.

2

The Turks Through History

The modern Turkish state has derived its distinctive quality in large part from its Ottoman inheritance. Unlike most nations created in the twentieth century, the Turkish Republic drew on long experience in managing its own affairs as an independent state. Its institutions were deeply rooted in an imperial past. Indeed, modern Turkey inherited a staff of administrators schooled in diplomatic maneuver and practiced in the skills of operating a complex society.

Turkey is today the land of the Turks. It was not always so. From their ancestral homeland in Central Asia, Turkish people began to arrive in Anatolia in the eleventh century. Thus started a historical confrontation with the Greek world that left a legacy that has troubled both the Hellenes and the Turks in contemporary times. Contrary to popular belief, however, this encounter was not one of unrelenting hostility over the intervening nine centuries, for, indeed, there were long periods of peaceful coexistence and genuine cooperation.

The "Turkification" of Asia Minor was a process of several centuries' duration. Turks came in waves from Central Asia, passing through the Iranian highlands on their way. They brought wives and children, yet their numbers were small relative to the preexisting peasant masses. The migrants had been converted to Islam during their odyssey, but for the most part they arrived as orthodox Sunnis rather than taking on the Shiite interpretation common to Iranian civilization with which they nonetheless retained the most intimate ties for centuries to come.

From the start of the eleventh century, Turkish tribes

from the Iranian plateau and Mesopotamia raided Anatolia as the opportunity presented itself. These tribal forays made no attempt to settle, but, instead, intended to plunder the Byzantine realm. After a major engagement at Manzikert in Southeastern Anatolia in 1071, however, the Byzantine defense perimeter was broken, permitting for the first time permanent Turkish lodgments in Asia Minor. Thereafter, the Seljuks, exploiting Byzantine dynastic rivalries, moved rapidly to found a state in Anatolia.

The very success of the Seljuks in quickly gaining control of most of Asia Minor made them a major target of the Crusaders, who soon cut them off from the coast. The end of rapid growth slowed the inflow of booty, weakening the economic underpinnings of the state. The chief obstacle to preserving the Seljuk kingdom in Anatolia, however, lay in its failure to resolve the problem of succession. This difficulty was exacerbated by the fractiousness of the Turkish tribes that originally formed the basic fighting force of the Seljuk rulers, forces that were never entirely displaced by the organization of a central standing army of slaves and mercenaries.

Pressing westward in the thirteenth century, the Mongols destroyed the Turkish army in 1243 at the battle of Köse Dağ. Although the Mongols ruled through protectorates, the Seljuks did not recover from this blow. Rival principalities took advantage of the general breakdown of Seljuk central power. Tribal formations increased in independence in the countryside, while social-cum-professional associations (the so-called *ahis*) rose in importance within the towns. As a result, by the early fourteenth century, the Seljuk Sultanate disappeared without fanfare, essentially falling of its own weight.

RISE OF THE OTTOMAN EMPIRE

The Ottomans were only one of a handful of Turkish clans vying for supremacy on the ruins of the Seljuk state toward the start of the fourteenth century. But they had the advantage of bordering on the moribund Byzantine Empire, which was preoccupied with internal feuding and conflict with the Latin West. Indeed, the symbiosis of the two realms, expressed in alliances and even the marriage of an Ottoman sultan to a Byzantine princess, provided the Ottomans not only allies against the Crusaders and various Christian enemies but also aid against neighboring Turks. Beyond this Byzantine assistance, the emerging Ottomans drew dynamism from the combination of absolutist administration modeled on Seljuk practice, bureaucratic efficiency and techniques inspired in part by Byzantine examples, and, especially, the driving will of a powerful line of early sultans. Although rules for the succession had yet to be worked out, save for the decade of bitter struggle among Bayezid's sons (1402–1413), infighting over the throne did not paralyze the state during its early years.

Against this background, the view that an intense commitment to holy war dictated the main thrust of Ottoman aggrandizement seems suspect. Lust for booty was probably a more important motivation for conquest, since spoils of war fueled the economy of the early Ottoman state. Dervishes leading bands of immigrants from the Iranian highlands to the Byzantine frontiers did serve as the cutting edge of Turkish expansion, but much of their impetus came from their desire to settle out of reach of secular authority. Even the propensity of the Ottoman rulers to take the title of *gazi*, a religious term for strugglers against the infidel, was significant principally because it emphasized the urban and nontribal orientation of the early Ottoman rulers. Indeed, the Ottoman style of titles differed from the frontiersmen's terminology derived from pre-Islamic Turkish folklore. In any event, religious zealotry does not accord with the record of the first sultans in dealing with Byzantium.

A distinguishing feature of the Ottomans was their gift for government organization. At the center, stood the sultan; around him ranged a hierarchy of functionaries. From the first, the system was based on the registration of the population and the regular imposition of taxes. In order to ensure the availability of administrators and soldiers needed to run the new state, the sultans assigned lands and other privileges to the ruling elite. In addition to the cavalry force of *sipahis*, who were granted the use of lands in lieu of salary by the state, the sultans, from the time of Murad I (1359–1389), the third Ottoman ruler, began using levies of Christian boys (the *devşirme*) from their Balkan subjects to fill the ranks of the bureaucracy, the palace, and the army. These slave troops, the Janissaries, soon became the backbone of the Ottoman military establishment.

Ottoman organization owed a heavy debt to Islamic models, but it was by no means a mere copy of Seljuk precedents. The central bureaucracy, certain social practices, landholding patterns, and the town structure reflected Byzantine traditions. The formal orthodox Islamic institutions of the center were challenged by Turkish tribal ways of the countryside, by the indisciplined and independent forces that had frustrated the Seljuk rulers. But thanks to more effective central government order, the Ottoman sovereigns managed to bring these tribes under control. The subjugation of the tribes did much to ensure the survival of the dynasty, although it did not end the contest between the classical Ottoman Islamic society of the center and the looser heterodox culture of the periphery. Indeed, many scholars have seen the continuing center-periphery tension as a basic element of Turkish politics through the ages.

The Ottomans administered the empire through the *millet* system of autonomous religious communities formalized by the sultans following the conquest of İstanbul in 1453. The Christians and Jews were "people of the book" and thus not subject to forcible conversion to Islam; hence the holding of various religious leaderships responsible for the routine administration of taxes and the general obedience of their flocks was a cost-effective way to govern. But this system contained the seeds of danger to the empire in later generations, when modern nationalism invested religious community differences with new meaning. At that point, the convergence of religious community, language, and ethnic identity promoted such a strong national consciousness that the flexible, decentralized units of the past became the principal divisive forces in the Ottoman Empire.

PROBLEMS OF DECLINE

Signs that all was not well in the Ottoman institutions and governing structure accompanied the end of the era of conquest. Following a series of ten outstanding sultans, culminating in the reign of Süleyman the Magnificent (1520–1566), the empire reached its apogee. Thereafter, the westward expansion of the Ottoman domain slowed dramatically. The Turks failed to take Vienna, which they besieged in 1529 and for the last time in 1683.

The causes of these troubles were complex, and decline did not proceed at the same pace in all institutions. Alterations in military technology that reduced the importance of the *sipahi* cavalry, a severe dislocation of the financial and economic position of the empire after the European discovery of the Americas, and shifts in landholding arrangements to adapt to these changed circumstances all combined to undermine the classical system of the first sultans. The breakdown of law and order in the countryside, the emergence of quasi-autonomous local gentry, and the marked unruliness and disaffection of the Janissary troops demonstrated the breadth of internal disarray. The increasing success of the European military forces against the Turks illustrated the external dimension of the debilitation.

With these structural problems came alterations in the conduct of the monarchy. Failure to resolve the procedures for succession hastened the immersion of the ruler in harem politics, to the detriment of national issues. But even when the sultans and their advisers sought to understand why the empire was being left behind, their traditional approach of trying to restore the institutions of the golden age of the past could not address the dynamic changes that were in fact responsible for the decline. Attempts to increase military strength by borrowing technology from the West encountered stiff opposition from the more conservative elements of the ruling elite.

However, nepotism and the inheritance of office, although they have often been identified as an important cause of the empire's decline, may not have injured the administrative system in a major way. In a society where educational possibilities were minimal, family training was an effective— perhaps the most effective—way to prepare for office. Indeed, favoritism toward relatives, far from arousing general resentment, was the expected behavior of a responsible person in the Ottoman system.

The practice of selling public office, on the other hand, did damage administrative efficiency. Rapid shifts in personnel led to exactions designed to recoup the price in the shortest time. But even guarantees of lengthy tenure might not have reduced the desire for instant profit. The fundamental problem lay in the prevalent Ottoman economic theory that the ruling class was entitled to consume the agricultural production of its subjects (*reaya*). Indeed, the philosophy that the elite should be supported by the masses motivated the Turkish ruling class well into the twentieth century and posed a lasting impediment to economic development.

The increasing weakness of the Ottoman state brought about what is known as the "Eastern Question"—that is, the controversy over the disposition of the territory lost by the Ottomans and over what lands would remain under the control of the Ottoman Empire as its power waned. Ottoman territory lay athwart important lines of commerce of the European powers and blocked the Russian dream of a warm-water port. None of the protagonists was willing to let another gain advantage from the Ottoman spoils.

The Eastern Question is often dated from the Treaty of Carlowitz in 1699, which marked the end of the wars triggered by the last Ottoman advance on Vienna. From the vantage point of the present day, this highwater mark of Ottoman expansion stands out as a clear turning point in the fortunes of the empire. But the significance of this event cannot have been unmistakable at the time. In fact, to some extent Ottoman tactical victories during the eighteenth century served to mask this strategic shift from the offensive to the defensive.

In regard to Muscovy, the Ottoman strategic defeat actually came in 1569, when, frustrated by the weather, the Ottoman expeditionary force in the Crimea failed to take Astrakhan from the Russians. This setback left the Ottomans with a mere protectorate over the Crimean Tartars. Yet for the next century and a half, the weakness of the Turkish position was effectively concealed by continuing Tartar slave raids into Muscovy that netted over 10,000 captives a year during some parts of this period. Moreover, the Ottomans, intervening in 1711 in the wars of the Swedish succession, were able to encircle and trap an overconfident Peter the Great and his army at the Pruth River in present-day Romania. Intrigue within the Ottoman camp, however, lost the opportunity for the Turks to reverse the strategic tide. Peter was allowed to escape after agreeing to such lenient terms that the Ottoman negotiators who concluded the treaty were severely punished on their return to İstanbul.

It was the campaigns of Catherine the Great at the end of the eighteenth century that set the seal on Ottoman weakness in European eyes. To retaliate for Ottoman involvement with Polish rebels opposing Russian domination, Catherine dispatched her navy to the Aegean, calling on the Greeks within the Ottoman confines to revolt. The Greek response to the succession of Russian naval victories in 1768 was indifferent. But by defeating the Turks in the war, the czars gained access to the Black Sea and the right to represent the Christians of the empire—thereby giving Russia an advantage in the race to take over the Ottoman realm.

Up to the nineteenth century, Greeks had been attracted to Ottoman service. In fact, the Phanariot elite around the Patriarchate in İstanbul was used by the sultans to rule the Romanians in the Balkans starting in 1711. As a result, the educated leaders of the Greek community were not overly receptive to Catherine's "Greek project," which envisaged a system of Balkan protectorates and a revived Byzantine state. It was the traditionally unruly bands of Greeks in the hinterland and the exiles in South Russia who eventually provided the leadership and manpower for the successful Greek independence movement in the nineteenth century.

EFFORTS AT REFORM

By the end of the eighteenth century, this external pressure and the growing disorders in the Ottoman provinces convinced the sultans of the need for a more comprehensive program of reform. For the first time, the leadership of the Ottoman realm sought not to return the state to its earlier flower of greatness, but to strengthen it by adopting modern, even Western, ways. The reform movement did not become full-blown until well into the nineteenth century. Traditional institutions were generally left to die on the vine instead of being replaced wholesale. But already by the reign of Selim III (1780–1807) the new approach was evident.

Selim's reform was typified by his dalliance with the so-called New Order Army. This experiment began modestly in 1791 with the formation of a unit of renegades using European weapons and techniques. Although the sultan tried to move carefully in order not to disrupt entrenched interests, his effort to expand the new corps nonetheless rather broadly alarmed the provincial gentry and the Janissaries alike. Selim thereupon abandoned the experiment, although he did so too late to avoid an uprising that cost him the throne and ended, for a time, such innovations. It was not until his successor, Mahmud II (1807–1839), abolished the Janissaries by a stroke in 1826 that a resumption of military reform again became possible. Significantly, Mahmud's new army was built on the nucleus of veterans of the earlier experimental corps.

The famous "Tanzimat" (reordering) reforms of the nineteenth century differed from the earlier attempts primarily in their scope and degree of persistence. Directed in the first instance at strengthening military force, these steps were basically aimed at restructuring the state by promoting centralization. Competing elements, such as the local gentry of the provinces, were brought under firm control. But in the process, the bureaucracy expanded its functions to assume responsibility for additional areas of life, including education and public works, thus providing new jobs. Moreover, the senior bureaucrats took care to guarantee their rights by inducing the sultan to renounce his power to confiscate their property when they fell from favor. Thus, although the Tanzimat began in 1839 with the Gulhane Rescript, a ringing promise to treat all citizens equally, irrespective of their religious community, it was the functionaries who benefited most. Indeed, the tradition of reform in the Ottoman Empire inherited by modern Turkey has been one of government-sponsored, top-down changes, often against the customs and desires of the people at large.

The reform movement had a foreign dimension as well. Sir Stratford Canning, British ambassador to İstanbul, influenced the drafting of the Gulhane Rescript. Although Canning was bent on promoting the Christianization of the Ottoman state, his most significant work was the reform favoring the expansion of commercial relations with Europe. Thanks to his efforts, the Hatti Humayun (Imperial Rescript) of 1856 promised that European investment in the empire would be encouraged. But this new receptivity to European financial involvement led the Ottomans to bankruptcy in short order, an experience that has colored Turkish thinking ever since.

Nationalism among the various religious communities presented the paramount challenge to the Ottoman state in the nineteenth century. The effort to forestall non-Muslim separatism through promises of equality could not deter the Balkan peoples from seeking to split off from the empire. The Greeks achieved their independence by 1830, and the Serbs launched a series of ever-expanding revolts in the early years of the century as well. Russian meddling among the Slavs in addition to Western Europe's awakening attention to the Armenians, Maronites, and other Christians speeded the growth of separatism and spurred ever-increasing foreign intervention into Ottoman affairs. By 1875, Bosnia and Herzegovina were in revolt, and Bulgarian restiveness had elicited harsh repression from the Ottomans. Despite frenzied last-minute efforts to head off war by the Turks, a disastrous conflict with Russia ensued. In 1878, the Ottomans were forced to grant independence to Montenegro, Serbia, and Romania; Bulgaria was to become autonomous. These results only added to the desire of others in the realm (especially the Armenians) to gain similar recognition.

The Tanzimat attempt to integrate the Muslim population of the periphery through administrative and fiscal reforms, however, enjoyed some short-run success. The middle decades of the nineteenth century saw the remaining nomadic population of the Anatolian plateau largely brought into settlements. The raiding of Arab bedouin in Mesopotamia and the Levant was also greatly reduced. Yet these achievements did nothing to bridge the cultural gap between the Muslims of the provinces and the increasingly Europeanized elite of the major urban centers; nor was a base erected to bind the Arabs to the Ottoman Empire.

As for the important question of broadening participation in the political system, the Tanzimat reformers could take only halting first steps. Local representative bodies were established; councils were created at the provincial and central levels to advise the rulers; and in 1876 this structure was capped with the elaboration of a constitution and the creation of an elected parliament, although the authority of the latter was essentially that of a consultative assembly. This body was evidently designed as the vehicle for the elite to ensure its rights, but the new system was not sufficiently entrenched to withstand the reaction of Abdül Hamid II (1876–1909), who was accorded sweeping powers.

The Tanzimat also spawned bureaucratic opponents, the so-called Young Ottomans of the 1860s. These critics, whose main activity consisted of propaganda against the abuses of the regime, were heavily influenced by Europe. Their unifying theme, however, was nostalgia for Islamic tradition and suspicion of growing central power (although they generally accepted the principle of ultimate monarchial authority). While the Young Ottomans have been regarded as a kind of lower bureaucratic revolt against an elite monopolizing the top of the power structure, they enjoyed patronage and protection from those who occupied high office. Moreover, if the Young Ottomans were frustrated at not reaching senior positions in government, it was not because these ranks were closed to men of their modest social origins. The Ottoman structure still permitted considerable social mobility, as evidenced by the rapid rise of the great nineteenth-century Grand Vezir Mithat Pasha from relatively humble beginnings.

It would be wrong to regard the Young Ottomans as essentially the forerunners of the Kemalists. Although the later reformers echoed Young Ottoman patriotic sentiment and criticisms of the authoritarian power structure, the Islamic cast of the earlier movement limited the debt of the Kemalists to this source of inspiration. In fact, the Young Ottomans seem rather to reflect the age-old quest of the periphery for greater autonomy from the central power, their reluctance to attack the sultan directly notwithstanding. And in this way, they appear far closer to the early nationalist opposition to the Kemalists than that directed to Atatürk himself.

ABSOLUTIST REACTION

The dominance of the Tanzimat bureaucratic reformers ended with the accession of Abdül Hamid II. Although he personified the culmination of the Tanzimat drive to centralize and to turn the skills of the West back on itself, he also stood as the chief impediment to the evolution of representative government in the Ottoman Empire. Abdül Hamid II never shook off the pall of the circumstances of his succession in 1876, the momentous "Year of the Three Sultans." Abdülaziz (1861–1876) had been deposed following a demonstration of religious students, perhaps incited by Mithat Pasha in May 1876, and he died in a mysterious apparent suicide in June; his nephew, Murad V, suffered a nervous breakdown and was removed from the sultanate at the end of August; Abdül Hamid II, who had intrigued to get his brother Murad deposed, was proclaimed sultan on the first of September. Abdül Hamid II thus came to the throne suspicious of the cabinet ministers who had extracted from him a commitment to promulgate the constitution as the price of accession. He was constantly concerned lest new intrigue deprive him of the throne.

In this frame of mind, Abdül Hamid II used his powers to suspend parliament *sine die,* once the deputies, who had the power merely to recommend legislation, began to emerge as a focus of opposition. He sent the powerful Mithat Pasha into exile and subsequently may have had him murdered. Abdül Hamid II eviscerated the mechanism of representative government and censored the press. He erected an extensive network of spies and informers, a development speeded by the discovery of two abortive plots during the year after the dismissal of parliament.

Abdül Hamid II's reign was one of great contradictions. Although he strove to keep out Western political and social ideas, he continually pursued modernization. The communications system was greatly enlarged, with particular emphasis on the telegraph and rail lines. Secular education continued to move forward as government officials and, especially, military officers were trained to become more efficient. Abdül Hamid II turned to the Germans, who were not tainted by prior imperial designs on the Ottoman Empire, to provide a military training mission to modernize the command structure and tactics of the Ottoman army.

The efforts of Abdül Hamid II to centralize the empire also ran afoul of the burgeoning nationalism of Christian elements within the state, especially the Armenians. Until the mid-nineteenth century, the Armenians had earned their appelation as the "most faithful" community in the empire. Armenian bankers in İstanbul funded the sultans in a mutually profitable fashion. But with the Russian drive into the Caucasus in the 1820s, the Armenian population of adjoining Ottoman provinces saw czarist rule as offering greater advantages. The formation in the last quarter of the nineteenth century of two principal Armenian revolutionary societies, the Dashnaktsutiun and the Henchak, added impetus to the effort to break away from Ottoman rule. These Armenian societies attempted to attract European attention to their plight. And when Abdül Hamid II responded by forming special Kurdish detachments to suppress Armenian agitation, a cycle of action and reaction began. By 1896, this process had led to the dramatic seizure of the Ottoman Bank in İstanbul by Armenian nationalists. On the whole, however, the effort to focus European attention on the Armenian cause failed, whereas the Ottomans retaliated with harshness. Killings of Armenians in Adana and elsewhere helped compel the Dashnaktsutiun and the Henchak to make common cause with ethnic Turkish opposition to Abdül Hamid II.

The regime faced critical financial problems as well. When in 1881 inability to repay uncontrolled borrowing from abroad led to bankruptcy, the Ottomans were forced to reorganize their financial structure to put about one-quarter of the public revenue under direct foreign control. In exchange for ceding the salt monopoly, tobacco sales, and other resources to the Public Debt Administration under a European directorate with interests in the Ottoman railway companies, the debt was cut nearly in half and the interest rate was lowered to 1 percent. The Public Debt Administration set standards for honesty and efficiency; it also paid regular salaries and reduced smuggling. Indeed, in the long run it contributed to the development of the country's economic infrastructure.

But the Public Debt Administration soon offended Ottoman nationalist sensitivities by expanding far beyond its original functions. Because of the confidence its management inspired, it was used to attract new foreign capital. The administration became the chief agency to promote railroad construction by guaranteeing payments to the European contractors. These railroads cost the Ottoman treasury an inordinate amount, however, for in disputes the administration usually took the side of the Europeans, who padded expenses and feathered their own nests.

The visible role of the Public Debt Administration as a revenue-collecting agency was also offensive to emerging Turkish nationalists. Turkish pride was especially injured when, in 1907, the sultan gave in to European insistence and allowed the placement of men from the Public Debt Administration in all customs houses in the empire to collect a special 3-percent customs surcharge. Memories of the humiliation of this extensive foreign intrusion into Turkish domestic affairs remain strong even today.

Abdül Hamid II's design required the weakening of rival power centers. Undermined by the Tanzimat land laws, the religious institution was already declining from its peak of influence in the deposition of Selim III in 1807. Although Abdül Hamid II played on pan-Islamic sentiment to keep the Arab population's allegiance, he continued to drain economic power from the religious institution and made no effort to improve religious education. Those who protested the continuing downgrading of Islam were exiled to the provinces. This treatment ensured that the religious establishment would not be in position to assert political authority when the empire finally gave way to the Turkish Republic after World War I.

The sultan displayed ambivalence in his treatment of the military establishment. He wanted a more effective army, but his fear of a coup took precedence over the funneling of significant resources to that institution. His spy system was particularly active in pursuing cadets. Indeed, this heavy-handedness may have promoted the very plotting that Abdül Hamid II wished to forestall. In any event, the military schools, with their enhanced access to European science and technology, became hotbeds of disaffection; the War School was even the scene of a strike in 1887. Shortly thereafter, a tiny group of military conspirators began to lay the foundation of the Committee of Union and Progress and to seek contact with civilian dissidents who had taken refuge in Europe.

THE YOUNG TURKS

Some authorities have suggested that the opposition that crystallized into the so-called Young Turk movement may have represented an important social protest of frustrated provincials or of those on the fringes of the elite impatient to advance. All of the original handful of military conspirators fit such a categorization. Even the original middle-grade officers who took to the hills to trigger the 1908 revolution appear to have been cast in this mold, as, indeed, was the famous triumvirate that ruled Turkey during World War I. Moreover, it has been argued that feelings of social inferiority explain the slowness of the Committee of Union and Progress to take power after the 1908 revolution. Yet the facts are complex enough to raise caution about regarding the Young Turks as primarily a movement of the socially disadvantaged.

In the first, place, *Young Turk* is a catchall term for the congeries of diverse elements of the ruling class who opposed Hamidian despotism. It embraced even Prince Sabahattin of the royal blood and Mahmud Celâleddin Pasha, brother-in-law of the sultan. Other prominent personalities came from long-established civil service or military families. Although a number of officials of modest origins were in the forefront of the Young Turk movement, they had already become, by virtue of their education, members of the ruling class with the potential for advancement to the top. Moreover, in addition to these members of the Turkish elite were Arab, Albanian, and Armenian revolutionaries who joined the Young Turk movement abroad, supporting common action against Abdül Hamid II.

What united these disparate elements was a political—not a social—aspiration: to share in power through institutions protected from the arbitrary intervention of the sultan. The common demand was for the restoration of the constitution. Steeped in the positivist approach of the day, the Young Turks of all hues universally expected that the mere liberalization of the regime would resolve their difficulties. Thus the various strains of opposition to Abdül Hamid II did not go very far in exploring their often conflicting aims for the Ottoman Empire.

The great diversity of the Young Turks dictated that those inside the Ottoman realm, who, perforce, worked underground, were not well coordinated. The military conspirators concentrated in European Turkey operated in separate cells in only intermittent contact with the emigrés. The latter were split into rival groups based in several centers in Europe and Egypt.

In this situation, the revolution came about by accident rather than by design. Fear of discovery provoked several middle-grade officers to revolt in 1908. But these conspirators, who were in Macedonia and well away from the capital, took to the mountains rather than moving on a key point. It was only after the assassination of the general sent to put down this mutiny that the sultan, fearful of further spread of sedition, capitulated to demands to restore the constitution. He did so before any Young Turk forces were even close to the capital.

Not surprising in these circumstances, the scope of the revolution was exceedingly modest at first. The military insurgents demanded only the abolition of the informer system and the restoration of the constitution. They did not ask Abdül Hamid II to abdicate, nor did they insist that one of their number become head of the government. Instead, the directing body of the Committee of Union and Progress remained in Salonika, far from the press of day-to-day government decisions.

The reluctance of the committee to take immediate control probably reflected more than mere feelings of inferiority of youth and of social status. The largely military-based conspirators were outnumbered within the Young Turk movement itself by adherents of the Liberal party headed by Prince Sabaheddin, and they were overshadowed by the prominent personalities in the emigré ranks. Perhaps even more important, getting control of the government had not been the agreed aim of the military plotters; they apparently imagined that merely to revive the constitution would be sufficient. Indeed, this expectation was widely shared within the empire.

The naive enthusiasm with which the revolution was greeted has struck students and scholars ever since. Amid the general rejoicing, the populace flocked to join the Committee of Union and Progress. Many saw adherence as enhancing their chances of election to the restored parliament. But although the committee's organization thus suddenly ballooned far beyond its original base in European Turkey, a small secret central committee continued to run it as a clandestine plotting group.

Elections in 1908 returned a very diverse parliament representing the major ethnic groups of the empire. Even the unity of the Turkish representatives disappeared under the competition of free elections. The Liberal party won in the capital; elements backing the Committee of Union and Progress ran strongly elsewhere. But this sharply divided parliament was unsure of its prerogatives and generally awaited the lead of the cabinet. For their part, the ministers, headed by a respected but aging statesman from the former regime, looked to the committee for guidance. The sultan performed his ceremonial task of opening parliament, but thereafter ignored it. As a result, the leadership of the empire was halting and tentative just when decisiveness was needed to point the regime toward clear objectives.

Government vacillation facilitated a strong reaction from

those groups that were disadvantaged by the revolution. One of the early efforts of the Committee of Union and Progress was to purge the armed forces, not of aristocrats but of the unschooled noncommissioned officers who had earned brevet commissions as lieutenants. These tradition-oriented junior officers had served to mediate between the commanders who had graduated from Abdül Hamid II's secular military schools and the rank and file who were religiously observant. The fury of the purged officers against the new regime was fed by the press, which within a few months became highly critical of the committee's moves to dominate the parliament and run the government. Because the Young Turk officers took little care not to offend the Muslim sensitivities of the troops, it was easy for religious rabble-rousers to inflame mutinous sentiment among the military units in İstanbul.

The 1909 countercoup was spearheaded by a military uprising in the capital. The indecisiveness of the cabinet allowed the insurrection to spread to most of the forces in the city and to elicit support from civilian foes of the Committee of Union and Progress. Although Abdül Hamid II probably neither provoked nor even abetted the mutiny, his continued presence in the Sultanate offered an obvious rallying point for dissidents. But as soon as the troops in the provinces, led by committee loyalists, could reach İstanbul by rail, the countercoup collapsed. This time, the sultan fell with the committee's opponents; he was deposed and lived under house arrest in Salonika until his death in 1915.

The departure of Abdül Hamid II was accompanied by a more far-reaching effort to reorder Turkish political life. The shock of the 1909 reaction led the Committee of Union and Progress to change from a military-dominated plotting group to an open political party. This process was of immense significance for Turkey's political future, as the committee served as a model for the Kemalist party to come. But the committee retained to the end certain features of its clandestine past, notably the firm control of party policy by a central directorate not subject to the will of the membership. Yet, despite a proliferation of opposition organizations, the notion that the ruling party was the only legitimate agency to mobilize and direct the citizens of the state emerged as a key idea for future political practice.

The committee, however, never fully resolved its principal domestic problem: how to ensure party control over the armed forces. In fact, the Young Turk period confirmed the status of the officer corps as a powerful, independent participant in the political process. Although civilians came to be important in the inner councils of the party, officers, of whom Mahmut Şevket Pasha and Enver were the most prominent, dominated the government after 1909, even when they did not formally occupy the top posts.

In these circumstances, the Union and Progress party was never able to ensure unity within its ranks. Committee factions broke off to ally themselves with the liberal opposition and with dissident military officers. At one point in 1912, this opposition coalition was even able to seize power, until Enver and loyalist units shouldered it aside some months later. Thereafter, a triumvirate consisting of Enver, Talat Pasha, and Cemal Pasha instituted authoritarian rule. Organized dissent was repressed and some opposition figures fled abroad. Although parliament continued to convene, it was unquestionably the triumvirate that ruled until 1918.

The major foreign preoccupation of the Young Turks was how to preserve the Ottoman Empire against rising pressures from outside. Starting in 1911 with the attack on Turkey by its Balkan neighbors, the Young Turks faced almost continuous military operations on various fronts. In this situation, their policy of promoting Ottomanism (which had permitted the incorporation of Armenians and Arabs in the Young Turk drive for power) soon proved ineffective. Efforts to treat all nationalities equally by such measures as subjecting all to the draft (heretofore restricted to Muslims) were not well received. Nor, given their unwillingness to share power, were the Young Turks able to overcome the burgeoning nationalism of the peoples of the realm through essentially administrative steps. Thus the era of good feeling that greeted the 1908 revolution quickly disappeared, leaving the Christians increasingly disillusioned with respect to the impartiality of the government of the empire. The combination of internal dissidence and external attack eventually proved fatal to the Ottoman regime.

With the failure of Ottomanism, the Young Turks moved toward a more purely Turkish brand of nationalism. Union and Progress party's central committee member Zia Gök Alp led an attempt to turn the empire into a Turkish state, drawing on positivist sociological approaches to celebrate the pre-Islamic Turkish past. In addition, the Young Turks espoused economic nationalism in reaction to the financial controls imposed by European creditors through the Public Debt Administration. They declared null and void the Capitulations that had given bitterly resented advantage to foreigners and members of minorities over Turks in legal and commercial dealings. But although Enver Pasha was a convinced proponent of assembling the Turkish peoples of the world in a single state, neither he nor his fellow Young Turks abandoned hope of keeping at least the Muslim Arabs inside the empire.

For all their failings, the Young Turks left a major legacy to the modern Turkish state. The Committee of Union and Progress was frankly reformist in orientation. Under its lead, local and provincial administration was reorganized, erecting machinery that was taken over intact by the Turkish Republic. Halting efforts at land reform were begun, although only the idea, not any actual accomplishment, that formed a precedent for the future. Intellectual and cultural advances promoted by the Young Turks pointed Turkey toward Europe as an inspiration for reform; at the same time, this orientation further weakened the religious establishment, whose decline was sealed by the failure of the 1909 counterrevolution. Education was a major focus of the Young Turks. New secular primary and secondary schools were created; education for women was promoted. Contemporary social science notions were adapted by Zia Gök Alp and others into an amalgam that laid the intellectual basis for the Atatürk revolution to come.

Enver Pasha, then minister of war, personally maneuvered Turkey's entry into World War I on the side of the Central Powers. In the absence of his pressure the Turks would probably have remained neutral. Enver was influenced by

Pan-Turanist dreams to expand into the Turkish areas of southern Russia. But he was impelled to act by the British seizure of two Ottoman warships then being built in English shipyards. When the Germans offered the Turks two cruisers that had outrun the European Entente fleet in the Mediterranean to take sanctuary in Turkish waters, pressure to support the Central Powers increased. And he unwisely precipitated Ottoman belligerency by ordering these two ships to attack Russian Black Sea ports in October 1914.

The war doomed the Ottoman Empire. Only in the Dardanelles against a botched British landing were the Turks successful, until the Russian revolution knocked the czarist regime out of the war. Turkish losses demoralized the troops and led to a sense of hopelessness. This war-weariness contributed to a lasting yearning for peace expressed by Atatürk in his slogan "Peace at home, peace in the world," which has been the byword of Turkish foreign policy ever since. This sentiment was primarily responsible for keeping Turkey out of World War II until its closing days, when there was no chance of becoming embroiled in actual fighting.

During World War I, the Ottomans lost especially heavily in Eastern Anatolia. As the Russians advanced into the hinterland, the Ottoman government, fearing disloyalty, deported Armenians from the border areas. In the process, large numbers died; others fled beyond Turkish reach. But the aftermath saw extensive depopulation of the eastern provinces and an undying legacy of bitterness and hate by the Armenian refugees against the Turkish people at large.

The cost of the war in the Arab provinces was also great. Draconian measures to suppress Arab restiveness in Syria left implacable hostility and a determination to be free of Turkish control. Farther south, the tenuousness of Ottoman authority was vividly demonstrated in T. E. Lawrence's desert war. British encouragement of Arab desire for independence made the defection of this element inevitable. And although the Turkish armistice representatives still had hopes of retaining Arab domains, time and imposition of European mandates over the Arab populace speedily destroyed these illusions.

Loss of the war discredited the Committee of Union and Progress. The triumvirate was forced to flee abroad, where the three were soon killed by their Armenian and Russian enemies. The ferment of defeat gave Sultan Mehmet VI an opportunity to assert authority, until the nationalist movement burst into a fullfledged struggle for independence. But the sultan's subservience to the occupying Entente Powers sealed his doom. In 1922, he too was forced to abandon the throne and flee.

THE FIRST REPUBLIC

Significant elements of the civilian and military elite refused to accept defeat. According to a plan put in operation by the Committee of Union and Progress, local leaders came together to set up organizations for the "Defense of Rights" of Turks in various parts of Anatolia and Thrace to resist Entente designs to divide the Turkish heartland. Turkey's emerging charismatic leader, Mustafa Kemal Atatürk, shared in this activity, but he did not create the nationalist resistance or direct its earliest stages. A "National Congress" of over fifty groups met in İstanbul in 1918 to attempt to concert the defiance of the Entente quite independently of Atatürk.

Kemal Atatürk's special contribution, however, was to serve as an effective force to achieve the unity and continuity that the resistance organizations desired but were unable to accomplish on their own. As the only general to emerge from World War I with an untainted reputation, he offered a rallying point for the otherwise fractious Defense of Rights associations. Using the military chain of command, even after he had to resign his general's commission to avoid being fired by the sultan in 1919, Atatürk constructed a national resistance organization based in the Anatolian plateau. At first he proclaimed that its purpose was merely to liberate the sultan from foreign interference and to combat the Greek expeditionary forces, which had launched an invasion of Anatolia in May 1919. Increasingly, however, this movement asserted its legitimacy based on the will of the people, a construct in which the sultan would become irrelevant. Yet until the parliament moved to Anatolia, after the British imposed a military occupation of İstanbul and the sultan ordered the deputies to disband, Atatürk was able to bring together very few delegates at the congresses in Sivas and Erzurum. Nonetheless, he boldly claimed for these small gatherings the right to represent, respectively, the eastern provinces and all of Anatolia and Thrace.

Atatürk was a brilliant military tactician and a consummate political organizer. These talents were essential to his success, inasmuch as the wartime parliament enfolded competing interests that were either eager to assert their own predominance or unwilling to surrender their authority to a single driving leader. Despite this continual sniping from his rear, Atatürk had to whip local resistance bands into a cohesive national army to oppose the Greeks; he also had to build a civilian government apparatus. Neither endeavor was broadly popular: at times, the masses had to be cajoled or pressed into national service rather than stopping with the defense of their own local interests. Some resistance leaders even defected to the Greeks in preference to submitting to Atatürk's dictate.

The struggle for independence against the invading Greeks was successful in the end. Overextended, with lines deep into Anatolia, the invaders eventually found it impossible to withstand the Turkish counterthrust. The Greek front collapsed at the end of August 1922; by November of that year, Turkish forces had entered İstanbul, although it took until the following year for a final peace treaty to be signed with the Entente to grant secure existence to the Turkish part of the Ottoman empire.

New Turkey was based on the predominantly Turkish portion of the empire. Atatürk adamantly opposed attempts to retain a far-flung multiethnic state. The only exceptions to restricting the new creation to areas inhabited by Turkish majorities were the inclusion of the lands inhabited by Kurds in the east and the abortive effort to keep the Kurdish part of northern Iraq. Because Turkish nationalism was still a relatively new concept, Atatürk devoted great effort to fostering a strong Turkish national identity. To boost pride in being a

Turk—previously a term of derision given to rude provincials—he sought to replace Islamic fervor by a civil religion of patriotism.

Under Atatürk's leadership, Turkey became a republic following the war against the Greeks. That meant defeating the remaining supporters of constitutional monarchy, an achievement in no small part indebted to his prestige as a victorious military leader and the precedent of the wartime parliament. Because the sultan had collaborated with the foreign occupiers, the elite was broadly willing to abolish the Sultanate in 1922 and then the Caliphate in 1924. These moves were so widely endorsed that there has never been any significant revanchist sentiment in favor of the former royal house.

Although Atatürk led the establishment of the forms of parliamentary rule, he ran Turkey as an autocrat. Stung by the fractious squabbling in the wartime assembly, he bridled at the prospect of similar opposition during the postwar era. Accordingly, he set up a political party under his absolute control and, referring to the Committee of Union and Progress as a model, used his new creation to dominate the political scene. As "permanent" (after his death, "eternal") leader of the Republican Peoples party, he manipulated access to political positions. He was able in this way to rule with a free hand despite the merely symbolic authority that the constitution accorded the presidency. He eliminated rival political organizations, starting with supporters of the caliph in the 1923 elections and the Progressive Republican party in 1925. The "opposition" Free party—his own tame creation, which was intended as a device to promote constructive criticism and to discourage laxness in the Republican Peoples party—met the same fate after only a few months, when it threatened to get out of hand in 1930. Thereafter, he sponsored a modest approach to a corporate state in which party and government posts merged. But this fusion of party and state led to the atrophy of the former and the clear dominance of the latter.

At the same time, Atatürk set modernization as an all-encompassing goal for Turkey. He concentrated especially on the elite, with whom he shared the fruits of rule of the new state. The legal system, the alphabet, folk Islam, as well as the Islamic establishment, male dress, and language all felt the force of his revolutionary zeal. The state secularized and unified education. With the exception of a few secondary-level foreign schools, the numerous non-Turkish institutions that had served the minority communities were eliminated. Railroads were extended to link and unify the country. And in the 1930s, an effort at central economic planning took place. Thanks to this determined leadership, the direction of modern Turkey has been identified with Atatürk personally. Atatürkism (*Atatürkçülük*), a loosely defined pragmatic approach to modernizing reform, remains the touchstone for legitimacy today.

For all its revolutionary aspects, however, Atatürkism represented essentially an evolutionary approach. Far more a political revolution than a social one, it was based on the Ottoman elite. The new republic was staffed by the Ottoman ruling class, which gradually expanded through the slow process of education and co-option. Social mores were adjusted by fiat at times, but no sizable group was expelled from the ranks of the privileged to create a nucleus thirsting to return to the old regime.

The autocratic style of rule that Atatürk practiced behind the facade of a one-party assembly could not long survive his death in 1938. In fact, almost immediately upon taking charge, his comrade-in-arms, İsmet İnönü, gave notice that he recognized the need to liberalize the regime. Hence, as soon as World War II was safely passed, İnönü resolutely set Turkey on the path of a multiparty system. He may have done so largely to fulfill Atatürk's grand design for political democracy, but he also acted out of concern to ensure Western support against open Soviet pressure. Moreover, he was well aware that rising domestic discontent would not have permitted much further delay in instituting competitive party politics.

A major opposition organization, the Democrat party, was established in 1946 by four prominent defectors from the Republican Peoples party. Headed by Celal Bayar, who had been Atatürk's last prime minister, this organization ran relatively strongly in the general elections, which had been advanced to July 1946 to catch the new party before it could fully organize. With a sizable parliamentary bloc as a sounding board to keep public opinion focused on their new party, the Democrats spent the next four years in grass-roots organizing. Surviving a major split by conservatives who broke off to form the Nation party, the Democrats united a broad range of intellectual, business, and peasant constituents from the more modernized parts of the country. When the Democrat party decisively won the 1950 elections, they profited as much from a protest vote against the arrogance and excesses of one-party rule and for greater democracy as from a positive endorsement of the new party. İnönü gracefully surrendered power to the opposition that he had permitted and even encouraged to form.

The Democrat party government did not usher in the hoped for millennium. This stage of Turkey's postwar democratic experiment was deeply flawed. Lacking a tradition of tolerance of dissent, the Democrats wasted little time in retaliating against their opposition. In 1953, the government nationalized the assets of the Republican Peoples party on the grounds that Atatürk's organization had benefited from state assistance in the one-party era. The Democrats also closed the splinter Nation party in 1954 on charges of exploiting religion. The ruling party restricted press criticism through harsh laws to penalize those whose writings attacked the moral authority of the government even if their charges could be proved. In 1957, as opposition to these high-handed acts mounted, the Democrats banned electoral coalitions in order to head off a combined challenge from the Republican Peoples party and the small Freedom party, which had split off from the Democrats in protest against their intolerance of dissent. Finally, in a move that demonstrated disdain for the democratic process, the Democrat party in 1960 delegated authority to a fifteen-man investigatory body to ban all political activity as it saw fit.

These moves were seen as threatening to the Atatürkist forces and as a blatant attempt to impose a single-party dictatorship. They thus sundered the constellation of progressive elements that backed the Democrat party in its quest for power in the hopes that democracy would cure Turkey's ills. The intellectual elite during the 1950s gravitated toward a left-of-center stance, revitalizing and defining a constituency that has shown itself to be a permanent feature of the Turkish landscape. As a result, by the end of the decade of Democrat rule, the division of the Turkish political scene into right-of-center and left-of-center major blocs had been accomplished. The Turkish political contest was ready to assume its current context.

THE SECOND REPUBLIC

Obliged to take sides when the government turned to the army to keep the opposition in line, the middle levels of the officer corps led a revolt in May 1960. The civilians readily accepted this move to impose military rule and end the intolerable political pressure of the bitter conflict between the ins and the outs. Yet the new junta had not agreed among its own members on a long-range program before taking power. An important faction, embracing the senior generals who quickly perceived the dangers of politicizing the armed forces, favored merely putting the political process "back on track" by erecting a new constitution and returning power to the civilians. The presence of İnönü (Atatürk's closest collaborator and a former general in his own right) as head of the party that had been in opposition during the decade before the military revolt also offered the officers an attractive way to surrender the reins of government. Thus, after dissolving the Democrat party and after presiding over popular ratification of new constitutional checks and balances designed to prevent the excesses of the earlier concentration of power, the junta allowed new parties to form, including the Justice party, whose very name suggested a demand for fairer treatment of the Democrats. This new organization was headed by Ragıp Gümüşpala, the first chief of staff appointed by the junta after taking power in 1960. His presence at the head of the new party was apparently designed to demonstrate its loyalty to the new order. The military rulers then held elections in October 1961. Nonetheless, with a former ranking general as president, the military remained an important political force. And the specter of the armed forces in the background served as reassurance that politicians would not be tempted to consider retaliation for the 1960 intervention.

The new political structure did not cure the intense political rivalry that had brought down the First Republic. Contrary to the expectations of the military rulers, revanchist sentiment animated substantial numbers of the voters, but the newness of the parties on the right of center prevented the electorate from settling on one unequivocal choice to succeed the Democratic party. The failure of any party to win a parliamentary majority in the 1961 elections raised the need for coalition government, a recurrent requirement of the Second Republic. İsmet İnönü's Republican Peoples party, with its plurality in the lower house, headed a shifting array of coalitions with minor party partners. This expedient provided weak and unstable direction, as partisan wrangling constantly threatened to pull the coalitions apart.

The 1965 elections returned a majority to the Justice party, whose leadership had been taken over by Süleyman Demirel, a civil engineer with links to the banned Democrat party. Yet the prospect of more stable rule reconciled the senior generals to the advent of this organization despite its ties to the previous regime. The Justice party enacted an amnesty for former Democrat parliamentarians still in jail and pardoned former President Celâl Bayar. The new government also placed its own partisan supporters in some of the top posts of the civil service. Although Demirel seemed relatively cautious in initiating economic departures, he sought to encourage foreign industrial investment during these years. Moreover, he was fortunate that Turkey's long-standing balance-of-payments pinch was alleviated by a rapidly rising tide of remittances from Turkish workers in Europe. Thanks to this unplanned and unforeseen development, Turkey entered an era of unaccustomed prosperity. In this atmosphere, the Justice party scored a second victory at the polls in 1969, thereby increasing its majority in parliament despite a slight drop in its proportion of the popular vote.

Demirel's most serious challenge came from the flowering

of leftist and rightist extremism in the permissive constitutional environment of the Second Republic. This growing extremism was manifested in rising student restiveness accompanied by political violence. Perhaps recalling the solidarity between students and the army that had been so much in evidence during the 1960 military move, Demirel appeared undecided at first on how to treat this turmoil. By 1971, an anarchist movement was fomenting terrorism and kidnappings that seriously embarrassed the government.

This mounting violence, which spread well beyond the campuses, aroused not sympathy but great anxiety among the senior military commanders. In March 1971, they issued an extraordinary public demand for more effective government to cope with the threat to law and order. They warned that "if this is not promptly undertaken, the Turkish Armed Forces will use their legal rights and seize power directly to accomplish the duty of protecting and supervising the Turkish Republic."[1]

Confronted by this ultimatum, Demirel immediately resigned. Parliament responded to this challenge by voting a series of cabinets under nonpartisan prime ministers and drawn primarily from technocrats. These governments curbed political debate by imposing martial law on important sections of the country, including all the provinces in which universities were located. The Turkish Labor party, Turkey's only legal Marxist party, was banned. These moves succeeded in putting down the terrorist movement, although political prisoners, some charged with nebulous offenses, filled the jails.

The effort to return to normalcy by holding elections in 1973 produced instead a standoff among the major parties. The right-of-center constituency, which had formed the main reservoir of votes for the Justice party, had fragmented badly; a religious party (the National Salvation party) successfully wooed the so-called prayer rug vote; a group of conservatives also left the Justice party in a factional dispute over cabinet representation. On the other hand, the Republican Peoples party was able to solidify its grip on the left-of-center constituency, especially with the closing of the Turkish Labor party, which had previously siphoned off votes from the left wing. When the returns were tallied in October 1973, the smaller conservative parties thus ended up in the swing position between the Justice party and the Republican Peoples party, the latter now led by Bülent Ecevit, who had displaced the aging İsmet İnönü.

The next seven years saw increasingly troubled coalition government in Turkey. The combination of Ecevit's party and the National Salvation party in 1974 took the widely popular move to end the ban on poppy cultivation imposed by the previous military-backed regime. Even the legal poppy trade furnished a high cash income to an otherwise depressed population on the western fringes of the Anatolian plateau. And reversing the prohibition even while imposing stringent requirements to keep farmers from lucrative illegal trade was regarded as a declaration of independence from the United States. The main accomplishment of this government in its nine months in office, howver, was to preside over the military intervention on the island of Cyprus following a Greek-inspired putsch against President Makarios. That recourse to arms inflated Turkish national pride to unusual heights and fed a heady gingoism that has persisted ever since.

When Ecevit resigned in September 1974, hoping to force elections to exploit this foreign triumph, the Justice party instead was able to form a government of the center right. The survival of this alignment for two and a half years demonstrated that Demirel had regained the confidence of the generals. Yet this center-right coalition was primarily a blocking force to prevent Ecevit from coming to power; it had no more success than he had had in resolving Turkey's urgent need for coherent government. The National Salvation party used its position to extract important concessions that limited maneuver on foreign as well as domestic issues. Indeed, the strains of managing this uneasy coalition finally led Demirel to agree with the Republican Peoples party to advance the date of the general elections from October to June 1977.

The 1977 vote produced another parliamentary standoff. After bitter parliamentary maneuvering, Ecevit used the lure of cabinet posts to secure the defection of nearly a dozen Justice party deputies to bring into being a government with a bare majority in the lower house. Despite its weak base, the Republican Peoples party cabinet took some steps to address the deepening economic crisis, even though it was unable to arrest the skyrocketing inflation. The regime also proved unable to slow the upwelling of terrorism. The pace of political killings by the extreme right and left shot up dramatically by the end of 1979 and political violence became Turkey's most critical national problem, sending shock waves throughout the body politic. Ecevit did extend martial law, which had been instituted after communal conflict at Kah-ramanmaraş in east central Turkey in December 1978 left over one hundred people dead. But his inability to halt the downward spiral of the economy, and especially his failure to alleviate the sharply deteriorating security situation, eroded his party's popularity. As a result, the Justice party scored major gains in the senatorial elections held in a third of Turkey's provinces in October 1979. Facing a continuing trickle of defections that had removed his majority in the lower house, Ecevit resigned, passing the prime ministership back to Demirel.

Although the new Justice party government tackled the economic crisis with great energy, accepting, for example, a radical program proposed by the International Monetary Fund (IMF) in January 1980, this administration was notably unable to stem political violence. The opposition ignored repeated warnings from the ranking generals to back the government in granting additional authority to the military to impose order. Instead, the National Salvation party appeared to sponsor disrespect for the constitution; Kurdish dissidence mounted in the east; and the government's existence was challenged by motions of no-confidence against cabinet members. In this situation, after five months of parliamentary deadlock caused by the failure of the parliamentarians to agree on a president when the previous incumbent's term ended, the senior generals ordered a military takeover on September 12, 1980.

THE THIRD REPUBLIC

Turkey's new rulers disbanded parliament, installed a government of technocrats, and announced their intention to return to the principles of Atatürk. Their first task was to round up suspected terrorists, and so they swept up tens of thousands of youths and seized a huge arsenal of small arms and explosives. But this time, unlike the action in 1971, right-wing activists were pursued as vigorously as those on the left. These broad arrests eventually brought terrorist incidents under control, although the complete elimination of their activities proved impossible. Nonetheless, the populace at large appeared relieved at the reduction of domestic violence.

On the economic front, the generals co-opted Demirel's financial team. Turgut Özal, who as undersecretary of economic affairs and state planning had been the major architect of the International Monetary Fund stabilization program, was brought into the cabinet with authority to put state economic enterprises on a pay-as-you-go basis, to promote exports, and generally to open the Turkish economy to market forces. Özal's success in arresting Turkey's economic decline helped increase confidence in the military regime abroad and boosted satisfaction with its accomplishments at home.

The leaders of the old regime, however, never appeared to have reconciled themselves to the advent of the military. Ecevit and Demirel were repeatedly put under house arrest or enforced residence in Çanakkale, and they were jailed for brief periods because of their continuing opposition to the generals. Moreover, their unhappiness over the procedures involved in forming the Constituent Assembly to elaborate a new constitution seemed the final straw in inducing the generals to abolish all the parties of the Second Republic in 1981. Temporary provisions introduced into the new constitution by the generals banned leaders of previously existing parties from participating in the political arena for ten years; parliamentarians serving in 1980 were prohibited from assuming leadership posts in new parties for five years.

As in the past, the military commanders soon committed themselves in principle to turning power back to the civilians. But this time, the generals insisted on a major revision of the system to prevent a repetition of the troubles of the 1970s. Thus General Kenan Evren, head of the military junta, supervised the construction of a new constitution, election law, and political parties statute. These documents reflected the desire to prevent political paralysis and to limit the participation of the extreme right and left in the political process. A temporary article of the constitution provided for Evren to become president for a seven-year term. Once parliamentary elections had been held, the four other senior generals who shared power in the military junta were to be reconstituted as a Presidential Council to advise the president for the remainder of his term.

In addition to erecting a new parliamentary structure, the commanders moved against the institutions they held responsible for promoting terrorism. They shut down the Confederation of Revolutionary Workers' Unions (DİSK) for publishing terrorist propaganda, organizing political strikes, and creating links to leftist organizations abroad. Other small rightist and extremist unions were closed as well, leaving only the largest and most moderate of the confederations, Türk-İş, in operation. To reduce the danger that educational institutions could again be used to incubate violence, the regime set up a Higher Eduction Council with authority to centralize university administration and limit the time one could remain a student. Finally, a number of professors were dismissed, thereby prompting about a tenth of the teaching staff to leave in protest or in order to avoid being purged.

Following these preparations, the generals relaxed the prohibitions on political activity to allow new parties to form for parliamentary elections in November 1983. This process was tightly controlled, however; the military reserved the right to restrict political competition in this first election. Using that prerogative, the generals limited the parties in contest to three: The first was the conservative Nationalist Democracy party, headed by a general known to be close to the military rulers; the second was the left-of-center Populist party, under a functionary of proven reliability; and the third was the free-enterprise Motherland party, led by Özal, who had left the government the previous year in disagreement with the military over how to cope with a banking crisis. Other aspiring parties were kept out of the running, apparently because they seemed to have excessively close ties with the banned major organizations of the previous regime.

Against this competition, the Motherland party won an impressive victory, gaining a solid majority in parliament. Özal had shown in the election debates that he was a skilled and attractive campaigner; his economic performance had earned him substantial confidence among the voters at large; and his break with the military suggested that his regime would represent a genuine return to civilian rule. Although the generals had evinced a considerable lack of confidence in him in the closing days of the election campaign, and although they even appealed to the voters to accord a majority to the Nationalist Democracy party, the military accepted the election results without question.

Özal lost no time in putting his stamp on the new regime. His first act was to decree more radical and rapid steps to inject liberalization into the economy than those he had tried under the generals. Although he carefully avoided offending obvious military sensitivities by acquiescing in projects to grant amnesty to those convicted during the period of military rule, he was not afraid to tussle with President Evren on political issues bearing on civilian primacy. Thus he used his parliamentary majority to overturn Evren's veto of a bill speeding up nationwide municipal elections in which political formations ruled out of the 1983 contests could compete. His judgment was resoundingly vindicated when the results showed the Motherland party to have run almost as well as before despite the broadening of the political contest. Özal also showed his willingness to confront military desires by permitting his party to reject a proposal to create regional supergovernorates, a project that President Evren was thought to favor strongly. On the other hand, Özal went to what the courts judged to be unconstitutional lengths in appointing his supporters to act in senior positions rather than proposing them for formal confirmation in order to avoid the requirement for presidential approval. His appointment of an acting undersecretary of economic affairs to oversee the economic program was overruled, and he had to add these duties to the functions of an existing cabinet member in order to retain his freedom of action.

Özal's decisive actions and his continuing popular support

promoted discord among his political opposition. The results of the municipal elections showed that the Nationalist Democracy party and the Populist party were far more artificial than was the Motherland party. Voters who had backed these opposition organizations in the fall of 1983 switched in large numbers to support both the Social Democracy party of Erdal İnönü, son of Turkey's second-ranking political hero after Atatürk, and the True Path party, which the public prosecutor soon charged with being a continuation of the Justice party. On the basis of their strong showing, these two newer parties claimed that they, and not the parliamentary opposition, were the legitimate spokesmen of the popular opposition to the Motherland party. The anomaly of a strong out-of-parliament opposition contributed to periodic agitation to hold early general elections without waiting for the five-year term set by the constitution. The apparent shift in voter sentiment to the newer parties also promoted continual bickering among all these minority rivals as well as competition to attack Özal. And in hopes of currying favor with the voters, some opposition politicians even agitated for changing the constitution to eliminate disqualifications of the parties and leaders of the former regime.

NOTES

1. The text of the ultimatum and explanations of how it departed from the normal procedures for official correspondence can be found in "Demirel Government Resigns," *The Pulse: A Daily Review of the Turkish Press* (Ankara), no. 1932 (March 15, 1971).

Mustafa Kemal Atatürk, founder of modern Turkey. His
piercing blue eyes electrified
his audiences.

Equestrian memorial to Atatürk in Ankara. The statue portrays him as a victorious military commander giving his famous order "To the Mediterranean" to drive out the invading Greek army in 1922.

Town dwelling on Roman ruins in Antalya. Traditional Turkish urban architecture included a screened balcony on the second floor from which women could observe life outside the house.

Banner on Ankara's main street to welcome President Eisenhower, December 1959. "Turkish-American Friendship is Part of Our National Heritage" is a slogan that might surprise the more jaded elements among current Turkish youth.

3

Evolution of the Economy

Turkey possesses the natural resources to support a highly developed and diversified economy. Its agriculture has the potential to feed the country's population with enough surplus to permit major net exports of food. Its mineral wealth, except for petroleum, is sufficient to undergird substantial industrial development. Man-made and natural tourist attractions abound; some of the physical infrastructure to accommodate a thriving tourist industry is already in place. Moreover, Turkey's population is now well on the way toward achieving general literacy and acquiring the technical skills, education, and entrepreneurial experience to run a modern economy.

Yet, despite these natural endowments of land and people, Turkey remains far from fulfilling its developmental promise. Today the country still stands at the bottom of the roster of industrialized states or toward the top of the ranks of the lesser-developed economies of the world. With a gross national product (GNP) of about $1,180 per capita in 1982, it ranks in the middle third of the world's nations in standard of living. And in the continuing sharp disparities between rural and urban levels of development, Turkey resembles countries of the less-developed world.

ETATISM

Turkey's current economic status reflects its historical experience. It achieved independence in the 1920s without possessing a strong native class of entrepreneurs and industrial producers. Trade, commerce, and manufacturing had all been

73

the special provinces of the minorities in the Ottoman Empire. Many of the more active elements of these communities left Turkey in the population exchanges of the 1920s or fled in the wake of the destruction of the empire. Thus, after a decade of independence, the Turks found their economy lagging farther behind the level of Europe than it had been two decades earlier. As the prestige of industrial and commercial occupations remained low, at least for most of the ensuing half-century, the most able elements of the Turkish population chose governmental or professional careers. That pattern has begun to change only in the past few decades.

Atatürk started with no strong doctrinaire positions on the proper route to economic development. Hence the first decade of the republic, during the time that he concentrated on consolidating political control, revolutionizing the legal system, and disestablishing Islam, was relatively restrained in economic departures. It was the perceived need to expand the railroad network that led the government to a larger role in the economy. And that course was given additional impetus by the obvious fact that private entrepreneurs lacked the capital to undertake major projects on their own.

Aside from these practical considerations, there was a set of psychological factors that pushed Turkey in the direction of elaborating an etatist system. From their experience with European financial domination in the late nineteenth century, the Turks concluded that political independence had to be complemented by economic protectionism and autarky. The conspicuous role that the Ottoman Public Debt Administration, which was controlled and staffed by Europeans, had played in draining off resources and in frustrating Ottoman economic independence left a legacy that still remains vivid in the minds of Turkish economic planners. And when the 1929 worldwide depression discredited the private enterprise system in Turkish eyes, just at the time when the Lausanne Treaty's restrictions on Turkish tariffs were expiring, Atatürk in the 1930s moved toward instituting a form of state capitalism centered on the creation of government-run manufacturing enterprises.

This etatist policy, underwritten by loans from the Soviet

Union, was instrumental in equipping Turkey with the rudiments of basic industry during the 1930s. But the development was uneven and incomplete, leaving the Turkish economy unable to function adequately once Turkey's international trade was cut off during World War II. The Turks were still far from able to break their dependence on imports to operate their nascent industry. Yet preemptive buying of chromium ore, of which Turkey was one of the few world producers, left the Turks with a large amount of gold and foreign exchange at war's end.

As a result of the impact of World War II, therefore, Turkey entered the latter 1940s with a severe pent-up demand, high rates of inflation, an eroded and inadequate industrial base, and an infrastructure insufficient to meet communications and energy demands. It was under this set of domestic imperatives that the Turkish leadership looked abroad to foreign assistance to fund imports to revive the economy. Moreover, the İnönü government exerted strong pressure to overcome the arguments of U.S. officials, who were reluctant to include Turkey in the Marshall Plan program on the grounds that its economy had not been physically destroyed in the war. The Turkish leaders were aware that their strong financial position was insufficient to rebuild their economic structure.

Even though U.S. aid pushed Turkey in the direction of greater reliance on private initiative, and even though Adnan Menderes and his Democrat party, which came to power in 1950, represented emerging business interests, there was no thought of abandoning the etatist policy. Far from seeking to dismantle those state economic enterprises that existed, Menderes continued to regard public-sector establishments as the engine of development. The Democrat party administration used this mechanism to reward political loyalists. Through tight control of imports, the Democrats exploited the system that made government favoritism rather than entrepreneurial ability the source of financial success. In the process, the value of Turkish currency was pegged at an artificially high level and heavy customs duties were imposed, thereby serving to foster the evolution of a protectionist import-substitution regime based in large part on quasi-governmental enterprises.

This economic machinery was entirely unsuited either for competing in the international arena or for the development of a balanced economy.

The economic policies executed during the Democrat party's decade in power did not succeed even in their more limited aims of ensuring political support for the government. Toward the mid-1950s, the weather cycle turned unfavorable and the marginal land put into crop production using the flood of tractors supplied by the Marshall Plan became unproductive. Turkey became a substantial importer of food. At the same time, disputes with the World Bank and the United States over the political orientation of certain development projects led to a reduction in essential inputs of funds from abroad, as these lenders refused to bail Turkey out of its growing economic pinch. Shortages of petroleum and other imported goods necessary for the operation of the economy slowed industrial development and fed a new wave of inflation. This downward spiral was halted in 1958, when Menderes, to secure a major commitment for foreign aid, compromised on his economic course and agreed to a deep devaluation and tax reform as well as some retrenchment in government spending. But the increasing role of state economic enterprises in the Turkish economy was not affected.

If anything, the overthrow of the Democrats in 1960 gave a fillip to the etatist approach. Many of the economic difficulties of the Menderes period, including galloping inflation and severe shortages of imports in the latter 1950s until the stabilization program of 1958, were attributed to a failure not of the etatist system but of planning. Thus one of the changes the military junta considered most necessary was the establishment of the State Planning Organization in 1961, with a mandate to prepare five-year plans to prescribe the performance of the public sector. And the remedy for Turkey's perennial balance-of-payment problems was seen as greater, rather than less, government regulation of the economy.

Successive governments in the Second Republic hewed to this statist economic approach. Under the regime of five-year plans, Turkey from the early 1960s to the late 1970s managed to sustain GNP growth at an average of between

6 and 7 percent a year in real terms—a substantial achievement. A major boost to this advance came from the rapid increase in workers' remittances during the 1960s, as surplus labor flowed to Western Europe in a flood not foreseen by the planners. Significantly, in conjunction with this activity, a class of entrepreneurs grew up who had gained experience in industrial concerns and who were ready to impart dynamism to further Turkish economic development once the development philosophy became more encouraging.

SECTORAL DEVELOPMENT

An important component of the economic advances made during the Second Republic was the substantial agricultural development that took place despite the opposition of many of the more doctrinaire planners who believed that an emphasis on agricultural investment would detract from the commitment to industrialization. The improving agricultural performance reflected the spread of irrigation, the introduction of high-yield wheat, and the slowly rising use of fertilizer. Dams on Turkey's major rivers built with U.S. assistance substantially raised the amount of land under irrigation. Mexican varieties of wheat, provided under a U.S.-assisted agricultural program, were quickly adopted in the better watered lowlands; other improved strains were introduced in the more arid uplands. These various developments permitted Turkey to go from being a large net importer of food in the late 1950s and all through the 1960s to becoming a significant exporter of agricultural produce by the late 1970s.

Turkey also profited from the fact that by the 1960s infrastructure investments funded by foreign assistance were beginning to contribute to Turkey's economic growth in other respects. Road-building projects, which created a network well beyond the limited trunk rail lines built before World War II, added a dimension of communications flexibility that has revolutionized the daily lives of the populace. Over the years, the new mobility has fed a large-scale internal migration of labor in quest of work, of untutored people in search of education, and of ambitious individuals seeking advancement.

In the 1960s, this migration branched outside of Turkey as well; at present there are nearly 2 million Turks in Europe, mostly in West Germany; several hundred thousand are now working in the Middle East. Of course, the roads have also let the outside world into Turkey's some 40,000 villages. But as a result, it is becoming possible for Turkey to create a national market and to permit the growth of new industry.

Tourism, although profiting directly from the revolution in communications, has not yet lived up to its potential in contributing to the economic upsurge. Foreign management know-how has combined with a largely domestic capital to fund modern hotels built in the largest cities to exploit the country's unusually rich tourist attractions; in addition, a growing network of smaller facilities was created, partly by Turkish investors and partly by foreign companies such as the Club Méditerranée, to lure, in particular, northern Europeans who wished to take advantage of the favorable climate for outdoor activities. But as Turkey lacks a tradition of operating such a service industry and particularly of organizing the ancillary facilities, many of these demanding clients have been disappointed with the quality of the services provided. In light of Turkey's inexperience in marketing and publicity as well, the flow of Europeans did not meet expectaions. And when terrorism began to disrupt the regular patterns of Turkish existence in the mid-1970s, foreign tourists were all the more discouraged from coming into the country.

By contrast, the industrial sector in Turkey has expanded vigorously. Textile manufacturing, largely neglected until the 1960s, spurted in the ensuing decade. Growing foreign sales during the period of the Third Five-Year Plan (1973–1978) spurred this rapid advance. Turkish products found considerable demand on the European market in particular, at least in part because of a move toward synthetics. Also important to this strong performance was the shift to the production of ready-to-wear clothes in place of the exclusive concentration on raw textiles that had characterized the past. Yet the imposition of quotas in both the U.S. and the European markets put a cap on these sales by the end of the 1970s.

Basic industry also developed significantly. Heavy industry had been accorded priority by the Turkish leaders starting in the 1930s with the British-assisted construction of the Karabük steel mill. The lure of becoming self-sufficient in the production of iron and steel proved irresistible to Turkish politicians, who saw the creation of an integrated industrial base as essential to economic independence. In the 1960s, Turkey used U.S. aid to build a second steel complex, although in the process demand for iron ore outran domestic supply. Nonetheless, the Turkish leaders at the end of the 1960s began constructing a third steel mill with Soviet assistance. This and other Soviet economic projects, most notably an aluminum plant and an oil refinery, were accepted in large part to reduce the substantial trade balances in favor of Turkey in the bilateral clearing arrangements. But the Turks ended up with facilities that have proven costly to operate.

The economy has also suffered from the failure of the petroleum and mining sector to meet its potential. The greatest disappointment in this regard was the inability to find and produce sufficient oil to meet the country's expanding needs or even to maintain its share of demand. The failure of foreign exploration companies to find oil in Turkey in the 1950s, when production in neighboring Iraq and Iran was booming, aroused the Turkish elite's suspicions that it was the duplicity of the international companies rather than an absence of petroleum deposits that had caused this failure to find oil. These suspicions fed a strong domestic political current against allowing foreigners to exploit underground resources of any sort, a distaste stemming from memories of European exploitation of Turkish mines during Ottoman times. Thus foreign investment in mineral production was stymied in general, and foreign oil exploration activity all but ceased in the 1960s.

The Etibank, the state economic enterprise that had been given the main responsibility for developing minerals production in accord with the prevailing etatist philosophy, could not fill the gap. Although Turkey was able in the 1930s to meet requirements for basic inputs for heavy industry such as iron and steel, subsequent expansion of this sector outstripped Turkey's ability to discover and produce the needed raw materials. After rising in the 1960s, production of iron ore stagnated. Indeed, none of the major minerals produced by Turkey showed strong increases after the early 1970s. Even metallurgical chromite, a mineral in short world supply, followed this same general pattern; peak chromite production was reached during World War II. This disappointing performance resulted in part from the etatist pressures to nationalize existing private mining enterprises.

ECONOMIC PROBLEMS

Perhaps the most difficult challenge faced by the Turkish economy was the persisting inflationary trend that dimmed the luster of Turkey's impressive physical gains. Periodic surges of hyperinflation in each decade since World War II led to cycles of boom and bust in the economy. The proximate cause of these inflationary crises was overexpansion of public-sector spending and excessive money creation by the Central Bank. At bottom, these binges of fiscal irresponsibility reflected partisan politics. Successive regimes used the etatist machinery in an effort to gain short-term political advantage. They wooed the peasant population by setting unrealistically high agricultural subsidy levels. They courted the urban dwellers by fixing foreign exchange and interest rates at artificial levels and by pricing public-sector goods below production costs. Heavy defense outlays to maintain the second largest land army in NATO and, at times, to compensate for politically motivated curtailments of assistance from the United States only added to the inflationary pressures.

An additional difficulty militating against price stability was the growing politicization of the union movement, which came into its own in the 1960s. The unions, all along, had exerted pressure on the government to favor industrial workers by raising salaries at an excessively rapid rate. But with the organization of a leftist union confederation (DİSK) in the 1960s, the forays of the unions into the political realm led to far more extreme disruptions of industrial and service industries than in the past. Politically motivated work stoppages and strikes became common in urban centers. Foreign-owned businesses were most often the targets of labor unrest, thus discouraging much-needed foreign investment.

The intensity of the Turkish commitment to industrial development behind high-tariff protection skewed the economy in unhelpful ways. Partisan administrations looked on the public-sector enterprises created by the etatist system as adjuncts to social welfare policy. The state enterprises were used to reduce unemployment by hiring excessive amounts of labor. On the grounds that these enterprises were models for the private sector, the politicians set the benefits and wages of public-sector establishments at unrealistically high levels. In this situation, as the state sought to market the products of these enterprises at prices below the world market, the resultant operating deficits necessitated ever-expanding Central Bank financing, thereby contributing to constant inflationary pressures.

The emphasis on industrial growth at all costs intensified in the 1970s, as the state planners redoubled their efforts to bring into being a self-sufficient, integrated, and comprehensive industrial structure within Turkey. They believed that only by acquiring such an industrial sector could the country compete with the industrialized European states once Turkey joined the European Communities, a move that was envisaged to take place at the end of the 1990s. As a result, since 1970 the rate of investment in Turkish industry has risen sharply and that in services has increased somewhat less, whereas that in agriculture has declined, with infrastructure investment remaining constant. Yet the production cost of products was such that exports grew only slowly in this period. Moreover, the disproportionate allocation of investment funds directed to intermediate goods instead of to investment goods, food, and textile products posed demands for large amounts of capital rather than creating broad new employment possibilities.

Turkey's growing industry was thus both excessively dependent on internal demand and geared to high domestic inflation rates. It also hewed to the interest of Turkey's planners in devoting more resources to the public sector than to the private, especially in the Third (1973–1978) and Fourth (1978–

1983) Five-Year Plans. The intention was to direct development to address such social issues as redressing the disparity in income distribution, attaining full employment, and promoting greater balance in regional development. These plans did not materialize as intended, however; the public sector expanded more rapidly than they had projected, and little progress was recorded in developing the economically laggard eastern regions of the country.

As a consequence of these various trends, the Turkish economy relied relatively little on foreign trade to promote expansion. Moreover, the Turks were encouraged to develop their internal market independent of the world economy by the belief that international assistance would close the growing gap between imports and exports. The establishment of the Aid Consortium in 1962 under Organization of Economic Cooperation and Development (OECD) auspices appeared to the Turkish leaders to be institutionalizing this mechanism. At the same time, Turkey's political leadership hoped that rising domestic production would reduce the need for imports.

Whereas Turkish politicians were ready to accept loans from international institutions extended for political reasons rather than out of economic justification, they were deeply suspicious of private capital investment from abroad. Despite repeated laws to encourage foreign investment from private sources, often enacted at the urging of the foreign governments that constituted Turkey's major donors, bureaucratic red tape and inertia foreclosed the possibility of a significant capital inflow. In an atmosphere in which the foreign exchange value of Turkish currency was rigidly controlled and did not reflect the high inflation rates that prevailed during most of the postwar period, investors had little confidence that they could repatriate their capital. And the hostility of the Republican Peoples party to foreign investment gave potential investors further pause. Thus the capital inflow into Turkey has been relatively small, although a small but vocal group in Turkey has loudly warned of the domination of the Turkish economy by foreign interests.

In this situation, once the world oil crisis had set in at the end of 1973, the Turkish economy became unable to sustain the impressive rate of real growth that it had recorded during the 1960s. Turkey's own domestic oil production had fallen to only about 20 percent of the country's consumption. As a result, the rapid rise in world oil prices in the mid-1970s left Turkey facing mounting deficits in its balance of payments, merely in its effort to meet the foreign exchange requirements for essential energy imports.

The quadrupling of oil prices at this time also reversed the demand for surplus labor in Europe. In consequence, remittances from Turkish workers abroad peaked in 1974 and within two years had fallen to two-thirds of their former level. Turkey's exports declined as well when the world recession hit its traditional trading partners, while unrealistic exchange rates for Turkish currency artificially encouraged Turks to import. On the world market, however, the price of these imported goods was rising in tandem with skyrocketing oil prices, thus dramatically accelerating the Turkish balance-of-payments deficits. Believing that the impact of the energy crisis would soon dissipate, the Ankara regime maintained its system of internal subsidies, which insulated domestic consumers from many of the price rises in the world market. But the effort to maintain subsidies produced huge public-sector deficits that, in the main, had to be financed through Central Bank borrowing. This, in turn, fanned the existing wild inflation, which exceeded 100 percent by the end of 1979.

The balance-of-payments deficit was met at first by the drawing down of reserves and then through short-term borrowing from international private lenders. Turkey's favorable credit rating, which had been shored up in the latter 1960s by the mounting tide of remittances from workers in Europe, was soon lowered. International lenders became alarmed at the sharp deterioration in the domestic economy and the terms of trade. Finally, at the end of 1977, the international borrowing window shut, facing Turkey with imminent bankruptcy.

These developments produced a sharp fall in imports in 1978, leading to major shortages in basic commodities and a steep decline in the use of industrial capacity. The GNP actually fell slightly in real terms at this time, whereas unemployment and underemployment burgeoned. The inflation rate far exceeded the maximum interest rate permitted, thus removing incentives to save and invest.

STABILIZATION EFFORTS

By 1978, economic conditions had deteriorated to the point that even the Republican Peoples party government, which had held to its strong autarkic orientation and commitment to public-sector enterprises, was willing to modify its stance to secure an International Monetary Fund stabilization loan. The program worked out with the international lenders involved a sweeping currency devaluation, a step that successive Turkish governments had traditionally resisted out of nationalist pride. Ankara also agreed to reduce the state budget deficit and to restrain Central Bank lending. The government even agreed to raise the prices of public-sector products. But after receiving the first and second tranches of its international standby credit in 1978, the Republican Peoples party did not follow through with the major tax reform inherent in the commitment to cut budget deficits; nor did it radically improve the performance of the public-sector enterprises whose deficits were straining the budget.

Nonetheless, a second standby accord was concluded with the International Monetary Fund in 1979, requiring further devaluation as well as implementation of the tax reforms and subsidy reductions envisaged by the previous agreement. Again, the Turks made an initial drawing, but they failed to satisfy the international community on the politically more difficult aspects of the commitment. Thus, even though the OECD group and a consortium of foreign private lenders followed in the wake of the International Monetary Fund in rescheduling debts and in providing some balance-of-payments assistance, these palliatives failed to stabilize the Turkish economy.

Faced with a continuing crisis in its foreign accounts, the Justice party minority government, which took office at the end of 1979, announced in January of the following year a more radical plan to reorder the Turkish economy than the country had ever before attempted. Former State Planning Organization official Turgut Özal was put in charge of a thorough-going program to liberalize the Turkish economic structure, dismantle the system of subsidies on energy and other basic commodities, maintain a realistic exchange rate, reduce budget deficits, and stimulate exports through streamlining administrative procedures and providing wide-ranging incentives. These measures, designed to reduce the pressures for money creation, addressed the International Monetary Fund's concern to bring down the inflation rate and improve the balance of payments; indeed, in its scope the new program went even further than the international organizations had been demanding in opening the economy to market forces. With its measures to reduce the advantages enjoyed by the state economic enterprises over private firms, the stabilization plan represented a basic reorientation of the economic structure away from the state-directed approach that had prevailed for the previous fifty years. Impressed by the new approach, the International Monetary Fund and foreign lenders put together a package of economic assistance of over $4 billion to relieve short-term pressures and thus gain time for the stabilization measures to take effect.

Implementation of the new program was assisted by the military regime that ousted the civilian government in September 1980. The generals kept Özal at the helm of economic policy. They enacted tax reforms and imposed greater restraint on budget deficits, areas in which partisan political wrangling had prevented the plan from being put into operation. On the other hand, the political change away from elected government alienated European donors and eventually led to a diminution of financial support from this quarter.

Results of the stabilization effort were rapid and dramatic. By the end of 1980, the inflation rate was declining sharply. Export performance had increased substantially. Remittances, which had rebounded after the 1979 devaluation, shot up another 25 percent to over $2 billion in 1980. Turkish contractors abroad concluded new contracts worth nearly double those already on the books in the first year of the new program; they almost tripled again in 1981 to over $9 billion in outstanding contracts, mostly for construction projects in the petroleum-producing countries of the Middle East. Each year additional contracts have been signed, bringing the total at the end of 1984 to over $16 billion.

The domestic economy was slower in responding to the fiscal and monetary medicine. Although interest rates were freed in order to permit a real rate of return after compensating for inflation, the banking system was not soundly enough based to cope with the challenges of reduced regulation without evident strain. Private brokers promising unrealistically high rates of return had siphoned off a large portion of the industrial savings in the economy. A wave of bankruptcies among these brokers wiped out many individuals' savings and called into question the soundness of some of the more aggressive banks. The resultant panic led to the ouster of Turgut Özal in July 1982 and a prolonged shakeout in the banking system coupled with a partial return to interest rate ceilings. The concomitant tightening of credit hurt firms that had borrowed heavily at the previously subsidized rates.

In these conditions, the amount of underutilized or idle industrial capacity remained high, although there was some improvement by 1981 as export-oriented firms stepped up activity. Industrial production dropped by 5.4 percent in 1980 but began to redress in 1981. By 1983, the real increase in industrial production had mounted to about 7 percent. This increase was unevenly spread over the various sectors; it was particularly evident in the automobile assembly industry and in the manufacture of nondurables. Total domestic demand, however, rose only slowly. Idle capacity hovered around 40 percent; it was principally the larger industrial concerns that responded vigorously to the stabilization measures.

As part of the free market approach to the economy, the generals in 1983 reorganized the State Economic Enterprises by dividing these institutions into those that provided essential public services and those that were operated in competition with the private sector. The former, henceforth to be known as Public Economic Corporations, were authorized to set their prices under government control to achieve public policy goals. Managers of the latter were to be accorded far greater latitude in pricing and production decisions with a view to keeping their enterprises competitive under prevailing market conditions. This reorganization was intended to boost the efficiency of state institutions and thus to reduce the drain on the national treasury. But its principal effort was to lay the groundwork for Özal's subsequent plan to permit public participation in money-making state enterprises.

Such measures did not ease the burden on labor, which bore much of the brunt of the costs of the government's deflationary policy. The regime sought to restrain the pace of wage increases to 25 percent a year or less, although inflation did not fall below 30 percent and even moved strongly upward again starting in 1983. A Central Arbitration Council was established to rule on wage levels in those industries subject to collective bargaining. Although dismissals of workers were prohibited during the years of military rule, strikes were *not* permitted and the more extreme union confederations were closed; the large, moderate, government-oriented Turk-İş was allowed to continue, although even its agitation for higher wages had little influence on the policy of the generals.

As for agriculture, its overall response reflected the weather apparently as much as the effects of the stabilization program. Indeed, the fruit crop in 1981 suffered from unfavorable climatic conditions; agricultural production in 1983, too, was hurt by bad weather. Despite its impressive past gains, Turkish agriculture is plagued by low productivity; it still performs at somewhat below the world average in this regard. A particular drawback has been the high ratio of fallow fields: almost one-third of arable land is left fallow each year, a proportion that is declining only slowly. Components of the agricultural sector related to export, especially market vegetables, however, did rise substantially; to achieve that success, hazelnuts and onions were planted on land heretofore sown in corn, thereby substantially reducing production of the latter. And perhaps as a result of faulty wheat pricing policies, Turkey actually imported wheat, despite a larger crop harvested in 1981. Overall, therefore, the agricultural sector improved only marginally under the stabilization program, running significantly behind the improvement in industrial production.

As is evident, the impressively favorable statistics on Turkish economic performance concealed some weaknesses in the sectors not connected with export activity. In fact, in the year preceding the 1983 elections, some general backsliding in the commitment of the regime to Özal's extreme liberalization measures, especially in the banking sector, weakened the still strong economic recovery. The lowering of maximum interest rates allowable in 1983 in an effort to reduce inflationary pressures contributed to a slowing in new investment. And the inflation rate began to spiral upward again in the last year of military rule, whereas exports dropped slightly from the high level of the previous year.

ÖZAL IN POWER

Coming to power with a healthy parliamentary majority after the November 1983 elections, the Özal government undertook to buttress the stabilization program with even more far-reaching measures. Overall, his approach depended on tapping new sources of state revenue and additional foreign exchange while holding down inevitable rises in imports and domestic expenditures. Özal was working on the assumption that by opening Turkey up to world market forces, foreign competition would induce Turks to produce higher-quality goods and lower prices. According to the Fifth Five-Year Plan (1984–1989) worked out under Özal's auspices, this recipe was projected to produce an annual 6.3-percent growth in GNP, with industry scheduled to grow at roughly twice the rate of agriculture and to get the lion's share of planned investment. Özal was counting on the rise of exports to bring down sharply the balance-of-payments deficit while aiming to hold the inflation rate to a target of 25 percent in 1984 and somewhat less in subsequent years.

To carry out this program, Özal operated in a number of fields. First, he removed the prohibition against Turks holding foreign currency and saw to it that there were almost

daily adjustments in the value of the Turkish lira, virtually
allowing it to float on international markets. The government
regarded these measures as a step toward eliminating constraints that promoted inefficient development and under-
cutting the black market in foreign exchange. Perhaps the
most controversial of the new program's features was the
liberalization of imports of luxury goods, which nevertheless,
were subject to heavy surtaxes. The revenue from this source
was to be allocated to low-cost housing with a view toward
reviving the stagnant construction sector, which Özal intended
should become the "locomotive" of development. Further, to
stimulate exports the program provided for a progressively
rising scale of tax rebates. Subsidies were also designed to
cover transportation costs in order to ensure that Turkish
products could be sold competitively on the world market.
Additional price rises were instituted for petroleum products
and goods produced by state enterprises in an effort to hold
the budget deficit to manageable proportions. Interest rates
were hiked to exceed the inflation rate in order to attract
savings. Wage increases for workers were restrained, whereas
income taxes on these wages were cut in partial compensation.

This comprehensive program almost immediately began
to show significant results in stimulating exports. Exports in
1984 totaled $7.1 billion, some 24 percent higher than in the
previous year. Despite the rise in imports to $10.7 billion,
export earnings covered 66.4 percent of import expenses as
against 62 percent in 1983, a performance that helped to
reduce pressure on the balance-of-payments deficit. Yet inflation remained high in 1984, peaking at a rate of increase
of over 50 percent a year before slowing somewhat during
the summer months. Cost-of-living rises bore especially heavily on labor as food prices rose more steeply than other
commodities with the liberalization of the economy.

But the longer-range impact of the Özal program was
difficult to predict with assurance. Reorganization of the State
Economic Enterprises to produce efficiency by paring down
the administrative structure was inherently a process that
would require time to show results. Moreover, it was too
early to tell whether the pace of imports would swamp the

increases in exports or permit a significant reduction in the balance-of-payments deficit over the longer run. Thus the Turkish economy—and with it the future of the Motherland party, whose success in the next elections would undoubtedly depend integrally on the success of the Özal program—continued to hang in the balance.

Petkim Oil Refinery in İzmit, one of three such installations in Turkey. These refineries process principally imported crude, as Turkey's production is quite insufficient to meet domestic demand.

Harvesting on the State Production Farm in Urfa. In the level fields of the north Syrian plain mechanized agriculture on large farms has displaced much of the traditional farming methods on small plots.

4

The Constitution and the Political Order

Politics has long been the preeminent preoccupation of the Turkish elite. Since Atatürk's day, generations of Turks have shared in political power and have come to regard their role as both legitimate and necessary to the Turkish governing process. Elections take place with regularity; governments shift with the results; allegations of vote fraud are both rare and minor. Unlike some of its neighbors, Turkey follows constitutional precepts with considerable precision, except in the most exceptional of circumstances, when the whole structure is refashioned anew. Even with military interventions (which will be considered in a later chapter), Turks over the years have demonstrated a strong commitment to restoring a constitutional system. This restorative trend gives the democratic order considerable permanence. Elected government in Turkey is what almost all Turks clearly associate with the legacy of the Atatürk reform movement.

Turks also expect that their multiparty structure will provide effective national leadership, responsive to the desires of the people yet capable of tackling problems decisively. While tolerant of considerable interparty bickering, the Turkish population appears to value order and stability; to ensure government efficiency, it also seems willing to narrow the range of views to be represented. Indeed, preventing politicians in Turkey from putting partisan advantage before the national interest in times of crisis has been a major concern of the framers of the 1982 constitution. The aim was to construct

93

a system that would operate fairly and smoothly, despite the politicians if necessary.

THE 1982 CONSTITUTION

The constitution elaborated by the Constituent Assembly in 1982 under these guidelines mandated a system that lay between the extreme concentration of powers of the Atatürk era and the elaborate checks and balances erected in 1961. The new constitution showed ultimate faith in the will of the people—in fact, more confidence in the common sense of the populace at large than in the wisdom and cooperativeness of the political leaders. Although the 1982 document was clearly closer to the 1961 version than to the concentrated powers of the 1924 Atatürk constitution, the current system provides for decisive remedies in times of national crisis. On these occasions, the broad civil, political, and social rights it details can be suspended in the name of national interest. In this way, the framers of the new constitution showed their determination to prevent a repetition of the ills that beset the parliamentary process in the years before 1980. Yet, in normal times, the primacy of civilian rule and the sanctity of human rights are established in law.

The 1982 constitutional structure is centered on a unicameral legislature. It was introduced in an effort to redress the imbalances in the previous two-house parliament that had so conspicuously failed to provide effective government in the period leading up to the military takeover. The current assembly is composed of 400 members elected for five-year terms. This lengthening of the legislative term by one year from earlier civilian practice represented an attempt to reduce the preoccupation with political campaigning that in the past had divided Turkey into warring camps of bitter political rivals. For the same reason, by-elections to fill vacancies cannot normally be held more than once between general elections, unless the number of vacant seats reaches 5 percent of the total assembly membership. If a prolonged or recurrent parliamentary deadlock occurs, or if a majority of deputies so desires, however, general elections may be held before their regularly scheduled date. The parliament's powers are extensive. The assembly has the right to pass legislation over the veto of the president; the prime minister is selected by the president from the membership of parliament and is responsible to that body; and it is the assembly that has the authority to initiate impeachment of the president. In short, the new structure is basically a parliamentary system.

Executive authority is explicitly subordinated to the legislative in this construct. But the cabinet can issue decrees with the force of law, if so authorized by the assembly for a specific period of time to deal with specified issues. The cabinet members are jointly responsible for the implementation of the government's policy as well as personally liable for the acts of their ministries. This provision was repeated from the previous constitution despite the fact that the factor of corporate responsibility, requiring the signature of all cabinet ministers to validate administrative actions, was used in the 1970s by the smaller coalition partners as a lever to secure assignments to government posts for their supporters and to block legislation that contravened their partisan interests. Perhaps to prevent a repetition of such tactics, the constitution also provides that the prime minister can take corrective measures to ensure that the ministers operate according to the law; he can even dismiss them when "deemed necessary" without showing cause, a provision first used in October 1984 to dismiss the minister of customs.

Another striking characteristic of the new system is the strengthening of the powers of the presidency, as compared with the authority granted in the 1961 constitution. Although Turkey by no means instituted a presidential system and the post of president remains largely a fail-safe mechanism in case other offices cannot carry out their responsibilities, the chief of state is charged with the vague mandate of ensuring that the constitution is carried out and that the organs of state function smoothly and harmoniously. To this end, he has been granted a limited veto over legislation as well as the power to refer constitutional amendments to popular referendum. Indeed, for the first six years he has the right to veto parliamentary proposals to amend the constitution;

his veto can be overridden only by three-quarters of the total membership of the assembly. On his own initiative, he can refer laws in part or as a whole to the Constitutional Court for a ruling on their constitutionality. He selects and appoints the prime minister and other senior administrative and judiciary figures, in addition to the chief of the general staff. He can call into session and preside over the cabinet and the National Security Council, but he is not accountable for their decisions or acts. Moreover, he has the authority to grant amnesty and pardons. Finally, if a cabinet cannot be formed within forty-five days, the president in consultation with the presiding officer of the assembly can call new elections. Assisting him in his functions, for the first six years, is a Presidential Council composed of the four ranking officers with whom he shared power during the three years of military rule.

The 1982 constitution continues its predecessor's provisions for a National Security Council. This body was originally created in 1961 to assist in "taking decisions and ensuring necessary coordination" in the field of national security policy in its broadest definition. The cabinet is enjoined to "give priority consideration to the decisions of the National Security Council." Thus the powers of this council have reverted to those of the previous period of civilian rule and are no longer the ultimate authority of the state as they had been between 1980 and 1983. Designed as a safety valve, the National Security Council permits the senior military commanders to communicate legally their views and concerns to the top civilian leaders; it also provides a forum for the president to speak in the name of the armed forces. Although civilian politicians did not always listen in the past, the National Security Council was often used during the previous period of civilian rule for the public expression of military desires; the force commanders who issued the declaration in March 1971 that brought down the Demirel government pointedly signed their ultimatum as members of the National Security Council. The military takeover in 1980 was also accomplished in the name of this body, after the civilians had ignored urgent appeals for increased cooperation among the party leaders.

An independent judiciary remains an integral basis of the Turkish system. Once appointed, judges and public prosecutors serve on good behavior until age 65. As an innovation, the 1982 constitution institutes State Security Courts to handle offenses against the integrity of the state, the democratic order, and the internal and external security of the country. Its judges are to be selected from the cadre of senior judges for a term of four years. Verdicts from this tribunal, however, can be referred to the High Court of Appeals, which is the final authority to review all penal cases. Superior administrative and military courts have final jurisdiction over cases within their competencies.

The system also provides for a Constitutional Court to rule on the constitutionality of laws and decrees, with the exception of decrees issued during a state of emergency (when the provincial governor has decree power) or martial law (when the commander has such power). Charges against the president of the republic and other senior officials would be considered by the Constitutional Court in its capacity as the Supreme Court. The Constitutional Court also decides all cases relating to the closure of political parties: its decision to reject the prosecutor's demand to close the True Path party shows the independence with which it exercises this function. Although the court ruled a number of laws and provisions of laws unconstitutional in the Second Republic, it has never used its impeachment authority.

Several additional administrative organs play prominent roles in the government of the state. The State Planning Organization, which continued from the 1961 constitution, fulfilled the general desire for more regular economic projections. However, the functions of this body have been less significant in recent years, inasmuch as the prime minister has kept the basic economic responsibility firmly in the cabinet's hands. Also over the past few years, rapidly changing economic crises have outdated plans almost before they could go into force; for example, the Fourth Five-Year Plan became obsolete within a year of its publication with the acceptance of the International Monetary Fund–sponsored stabilization program. In any event, the means for meshing the Planning Organization composed of technocrats with the politicians heading the government has never been clearly worked out. Özal has attempted to foster the necessary cooperation through the expedient of appointing his younger brother to a senior Planning Organization post in June 1984. Moreover, to emphasize the subordination of this organization to the political leaders, the findings of the Planning Organization require parliamentary approval to go into force. Its plans, once approved, are prescriptive for the government sector, but only descriptive for the private sector.

An innovation from the period of military rule that affects political behavior is the Higher Education Council, which is mandated by the new constitution. This body is designed to provide central supervision of the various institutions of higher education to ensure that they operate in conformity with the objectives and principles set forth by law. This council, which had been established in 1981 under İhsan Doğramacı, a forceful academic politician, was accorded extensive authority to appoint university governing boards, which in the past had been elected by the professors of the institutions involved. The Higher Education Council enjoys the right to transfer or suspend those in the teaching cadre whom it considers not to be functioning at a suitable level. Using this discretion, the council purged the universities in the last days of the military regime, dismissing some professors and intimidating many others into resigning.

The interest of the drafters of the constitution in preventing social strife is reflected in the provisions regulating labor activities. Although the right to form unions without prior permission is recognized for all workers, and although management may likewise set up employers' organizations, labor groups are prohibited from extending their activities beyond economic and social matters. They are also expressly forbidden to pursue a political cause or to have ties to a political party. Although strikes are legal, the union shop is not, nor can labor action be carried on "to the detriment of society." Collective bargaining is also permitted, but it is subject to extensive government supervision. From these limitations, it is clear that there will be no return to the free-wheeling labor practices of the pre-1980 period.

THE PARTY SYSTEM

As in the past, well-organized political parties are integral to the operation of Turkey's parliamentary system under the new constitution. Almost all of the parties of the First and Second Republics in Turkey derived from Atatürk's original Republican Peoples party, which after World War II split principally into right-of-center and left-of-center offshoots. The constituencies that supported these two main contenders for power still survive, but what organizations will represent them when the dust of the transition period settles is not yet clear. Increasingly over the past decade, the swing vote of the center of the political spectrum has emerged as the determining factor of electoral success; consequently, the contest for control of this key element has become the focus of political rivalry.

The Motherland party has thus far demonstrated the strongest claim to predominance over the right-of-center voting bloc. Its profile in the 1983 elections shows that it is an amalgam of important elements of the former Justice party, the National Salvation party, and the Nationalist Action party rather than a successor to the Justice party alone. Its heart lies in central Anatolia, not in the Aegean provinces that provided the base of support for the Justice party. It seems likely, however, that many of the voters in the major cities who gave the Motherland party its absolute majority in the municipal elections did so as a vote of confidence in Özal's economic approach and would shift elsewhere if his economic program falters. Up to now, his party has been built on momentum and expectations, not on established tradition; hence the loyalty of its adherents may not run deep.

The True Path party is the most active challenger to the Motherland party for the allegiance of the right-of-center constituency. The former organization has benefited from a whispering campaign alleging that its initials in Turkish (DYP)

100

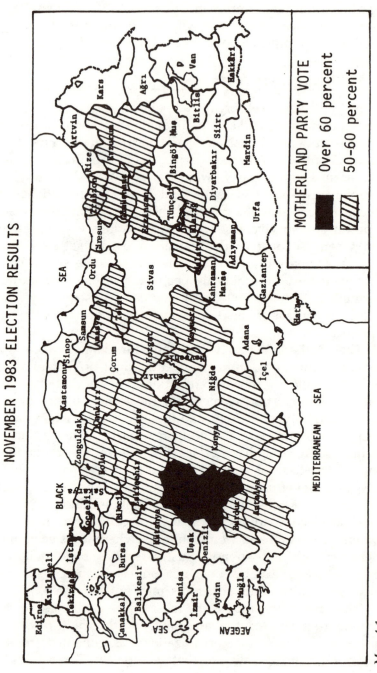

Map 4.1

signify "Demirel's New Party" (*Demirel'in Yeni Partisi*) and, thus, that it is the rightful successor to the Justice party. Polls in October 1984 by several Turkish opinion-monitoring organizations, whose previous sampling had been reasonably validated by the results of the municipal elections, indicated, however, that the True Path party had not gained significantly in strength since these contests. These findings also suggest that the Nationalist Democracy party, which is competing for some of the same voters, has declined to the point that its long-term survival appears questionable.

The left-of-center constituency seems to be on the way to becoming dominated by a single organization, the Social Democracy party. In the past, the left-of-center vote rarely exceeded 40 percent of the total electorate. The Social Democracy party commands only about two-thirds of this bloc, as shown in the municipal elections; moreover, opinion sampling at the end of 1984 indicates that this party still has not consolidated its hold on the whole left-of-center vote. Yet the tendency to go with a major contender rather than to waste votes on a minor party may help this party in the future. The Social Democracy party considers itself akin to a European social democratic party in outlook; it has staked out this position clearly in its criticisms of the Motherland party's economic policies.

The other rival for the allegiance of the left of center is the Populist party. Its profile in the 1983 general elections was reminiscent of a diminished Republican Peoples party— that is, one lacking the support of the major cities and the southwest provinces, which in 1977 had provided the basic strength of Ecevit's organization. The Populist party, however, lost much of its electoral support in the municipal elections; it is no longer generally regarded as the natural home of the voters of the old Republican Peoples party. Rather, it is now under heavy and continuing pressure to merge with the Social Democracy party to reunite the traditional left of center.

One additional small organization, the Prosperity party, stands in the shadow of the right-of-center aspirants. It has subtly advanced its bid to succeed the National Salvation party of the previous civilian regime. In February 1984, when the party was getting off the ground, fourteen former deputies joined its ranks in a well-publicized ceremony. At least half of these figures had at one time served as deputies representing the National Salvation party. At the party's anniversary meeting in August 1984, its major slogans attacked Western cultural imperialism and urged the audience to follow the "Truth" (i.e., Islam). Thus, despite the fact that the organization did not contravene the constitution by specifically advocating Islamic orthodoxy, its appeal to the prayer rug constituency of the National Salvationists was unmistakable.

The new political parties law is designed to reduce the danger of politicization of Turkey and to prevent as far as possible the formation of sectional or limited-issue parties. Political organizations are enjoined against promoting the class, religion, race, or language distinctions of one group over another. They can have no international ties. They are not allowed to advocate repeal of the basic secular reformist laws of the Atatürk era, nor can they promote disrespect for Atatürk or exploit his name or picture in party literature. Finally, they cannot question the legitimacy of the 1980 military takeover.

Beyond general conformity to Kemalist principles, in order to be eligible to begin operations political bodies must present a slate of at least thirty founding members, double the number required in the past. Before a party can enter national elections, it must complete its organization in one-third of the districts (including the provincial capital) in more than half of Turkey's sixty-seven provinces. On the other hand, to reduce the opportunity for partisan quarreling, the new law (as with the previous one) does not authorize the formation of party units at the village or subdistrict level, although members can be enrolled in these localities. Moreover, the statute has banned the formation of youth or women's branches and upped the age to join a party to 21. Parties may not engage in military training or have paramilitary adjuncts as did the Nationalist Action party in the 1970s. To guard against the partisanship in administration seen before 1980, the constitution prohibits professors, civil servants, and members of the armed forces from becoming members of political bodies.

Members of political parties were accorded rights that dilute the power of the national leadership both to determine candidates for office and, in general, to dominate the party. The new law provides for judicial supervision of internal party elections which are to be conducted by secret ballot. The party chairman is to be elected by a majority of the delegates to the party convention; the chairman is limited to six successive terms of up to two years each in office; and heads of province and district levels of the organization are limited to five successive terms of up to two years each. All leaders completing the maximum terms of service must remain out of office for four years before being eligible for election to these positions again. Moreover, in parliamentary caucuses, binding decisions can be taken only by a vote of the party's deputies, not by decision of the national leadership as in the past. The new law also restricts the right of the national headquarters to place candidates on the ticket to 5 percent of the posts in contest, and limits the freedom to put such candidates on the list ahead of those who performed well in party primaries. There can, however, be no public election campaigning for party primaries; only biographical statements can be distributed by the party, and speeches can be given only at informal meetings of party members. Even at such gatherings, no attacks on the personalities of other candidates are permitted.

The mechanism for funding party activity has also been amended with a view to limiting the power of special-interest groups. Donations are restricted in amount to 1 million lira (less than $3,000 by mid-1984 exchange rates), and deputies may not contribute more than their salaries to their parties. The requirement of heavy payments for the privilege of running as candidates had been a standard practice for some parties in the past. Although political organizations are permitted to hold fund-raising events, they are not allowed to borrow money from unions or from bodies that are banned from having political connections. Separate legislation passed by the assembly in 1984 echoes the past in according state aid to parties in the total amount of 1/5,000th of the national budget for the previous year. Parties that elected deputies are eligible to receive support payments in proportion to the votes they received in the latest general election. However, because the Motherland party agreed that the field was excessively limited in 1983 by the military regime, Özal's deputies made sure that the bill provided that parties that took part in the 1984 municipal elections were also included in the money-sharing arrangements.

State aid is thus likely to be the main source of revenue for successful parties in the future. But two kinds of parties could be disadvantaged by these provisions. On the one hand, parties created by a merger in which both organizations were abolished would no longer qualify for state assistance until after elections in which they gained representation in parliament. On the other hand, small left-wing parties, should they eventually come into being, would also be put at a disadvantage by this provision. They would have little chance of qualifying for state aid by electing deputies. At the same time, the legal prohibition against receiving political contributions from labor unions would close off the most obvious natural source of funds for such parties.

ELECTORAL ENGINEERING

Turkey's electoral constituencies are based on the province. But, as an innovation, the latest election law provides that in the larger provinces where the number of deputies to be chosen exceeds seven, separate electoral districts are to be formed within the province to ensure that no more than that number of seats is in contest in any district. The number of deputies to be elected currently ranges from two in sparsely populated Hakkâri to the thirty-six of İstanbul divided into six electoral districts. In fact, the design of the present electoral system favors rural provinces to a degree by reducing the relative weight of the major cities from what it had been under the formula that operated in the Second Republic. That reduction apparently reflects a desire to ensure the overrepresentation in parliament of more conservative elements.

Anyone not constitutionally barred from being a candidate may run for election either on a party ticket or as an independent. But the electoral system in Turkey operates to the manifest advantage of organized parties. Independents suffer from the provision that voters are limited to choosing only one independent; those electors who avail themselves of this option lose the right to mark their ballots for any other candidates, thereby necessarily wasting part of their electoral mandate. Otherwise, voting is by straight party ticket, a fact that makes party affiliation a distinct benefit, particularly in the more populous districts. Thus, although independent candidates received just over 1 percent of the total vote nationwide in 1983, these votes were so dispersed that no independent not running on a party's slate came within hailing distance of qualifying for election. However, four prominent personalities, including the prime minister and the defense minister from the period of military rule, secured the hospitality of a place on the list of the Nationalist Democracy party without joining that party and as a result were able to be elected.

In the Third Republic, as in the Second, Turkey's election law continues to be based on proportional representation. The current version of the d'Hondt system for allocating votes through proportional representation has been adapted to favor, even more than in the past, the larger parties at the expense of the others. To increase the odds in favor of the largest party, a new requirement has been imposed such that to qualify for any seats a party must receive more than 10 percent of the total nationwide vote. Moreover, in order to be eligible for seats in an electoral district, a party or an independent (who does not face the nationwide vote barrier) must win more votes than the quotient of the number of valid votes cast in that district divided by the number of seats to be awarded. Inasmuch as the votes of a party or independent that do not exceed applicable barriers are ignored, the proportion of deputies due the largest party in a province increases significantly if there are parties that do not cross these thresholds. For that reason, in the 1983 elections under the combined national and provincial barrier system, the

Motherland party got thirty-one additional seats beyond its proportion of the total vote. Indeed, with only 45 percent of the votes, the Motherland party won some 53 percent of the seats in parliament. Had the current system been used in the 1977 elections, its provisions would have ensured a majority for a single party instead of the mere plurality actually secured by the Republican Peoples party, as the 10-percent national barrier would have ruled out any seat distribution to all of the minor parties.

Under the present system of proportional representation, the position of a candidate on the party slate becomes a major determinant of electoral success. Candidates are to be placed on the list through primary contests in which voting is confined to the membership of the party in each electoral district. Statistics on the formal membership of the parties are published only rarely. The Social Democracy party claimed 123,000 registered members at the time of its first national convention in July 1984. The number of members of the other parties is also evidently small relative to the eligible electorate. In fact, in many provinces, the number of primary electors appears to consist largely of professional politicians representing local interests. Although the right of the national headquarters to place its nominees on the ticket is limited to 5 percent of the candidates nationwide, the leadership can put its choices at the head of the list, a privilege widely used in the 1983 contests to ensure the election of party founders in the larger provinces, where, in the case of the major parties, a top spot virtually ensures election. In subsequent elections, at which time the primary system will be in operation, this authority will be further limited by the prohibition against giving a higher position on the list than those of locally selected figures who receive at least three-quarters of the primary vote. Furthermore, the party leaders are prohibited from making deals to put those who switch parties on the party's ticket unless the new adherents win in a primary.

Except for the 1983 elections, during which time the national headquarters was allowed to nominate the entire slate, voters in general elections can use a complicated mechanism to indicate individual preferences among a party's nominees. In theory, that would allow the electorate to select the candidates directly, irrespective of their position on the ticket. In future contests, parties are obliged to nominate twice as many candidates as there are seats. But for the voters to exercise a preference, at least 25 percent of the ballots for the party must contain preference marks and the voters must not mark either a greater or lesser number than the exact number of seats to be awarded in the voting district. Otherwise, the ballot is considered simply a vote for the party slate as a whole. Although this last provision is likely to avoid the invalidation of a significant number of party votes, as has happened when preference marks were tried in the past, this procedure will probably prove too cumbersome to be effective in changing the order of candidates. Indeed, it appears to be merely a symbolic bow to the will of the people.

In the past, interest groups have played an active, though not always constructive, political role. Even though unions were formally prohibited from political affiliation in the Second Republic, parties exerted efforts to gain the informal support of labor confederations. Because the Confederation of Revolutionary Workers' Unions (DİSK) was thought to have contributed to political strikes and to have had ties with suspect groups abroad, the military rulers saw to it that the restrictions on labor engaging in political activity were strengthened. Whether that ban will remain effective over the long run cannot yet be forecast with assurance. But, as in the past, there will obviously be temptation by both parties and unions to erode this prohibition over time.

There appears to be little chance that political activity by student organizations will soon be allowed to resume. These bodies served nationalist causes until the 1960s and were generally supportive of the regime. Thereafter, they became drawn further into the political contest, focusing on social issues, economic development, and Turkey's international orientation. But discontent with this relatively tame activity led student radicals to break off in a rash of revolutionary organizations of the left and right. Out of this process grew the terrorist groups that turned campuses into battlegrounds and provoked the military ultimatum of 1971.

The imposition of martial law at that time curbed this political violence. But the government action did not directly address underlying social and economic causes of disorder, nor did it prevent a resurgence of anarchist and left-wing radical organizations following the lifting of martial law in 1973 and the amnesty of radicals in 1974. These splinter groups maintained more or less direct connections with the mushrooming extreme socialist parties that sprang up in Turkey in the 1970s. They were complemented on the right by the so-called Commandos of the Nationalist Action party, who at times enjoyed discreet government encouragement. The baleful role played by these various organizations in the descent into violence and the continuing arrests of young conspirators possessing stocks of arms and ammunition make the university age group appear the most difficult to control in Turkey. Under these circumstances, it will clearly be a long time before the authorities are willing to ease the tight restrictions on the political activities of youth, despite the interest of some politicians in lowering the voting age.

Voting in Ankara. Ballots are cast and counted manually. There have been no alleged significant instances of vote fraud since 1957. Interest in voting has risen to the point that over 92% of the electorate voted in the 1983 national elections.

The National Assembly building in Ankara. This building originally housed both the Senate and Lower House. Today it is larger than necessary for the one-house parliament.

Parliament in session. Atatürk's slogan, "Sovereignty Belongs without Let or Hindrance to the Nation," adorns the wall behind the podium.

5

Political Dynamics

Despite military interventions, the patterns of politics in Turkey demonstrate remarkable continuity. Turkish political culture has proven resistant to change. The conduct of party leaders, voting behavior, and the issues under contention in Turkey all betray a large debt to the past.

In part, this persistence is a reflection of the fact that Turkish political parties are not emanations of charismatic personalities but, in the broadest sense, represent aggregations with differing general approaches to social issues. For example, over the nearly forty years of multiparty competition, the Republican Peoples party became firmly identified with policies stressing government intervention to promote social justice while promoting industrialization. Thus the party could survive the death of Atatürk, a truly charismatic figure, and continue under lesser lights to command the allegiance of the reform-minded, secularly oriented elements of the population.

Similarly, the Democrat party's leadership could be lopped off by military intervention in 1960, but the lower levels of the organization were able to reconstitute themselves, after only a short delay, as the Justice party, appealing to the same voters who desired material advance but without social reform. The Justice Party founder, General Ragıp Gümüşpala, never ceased to be a political outsider; he also lacked a commanding personality. But the identification of his organization with the political approach of its predecessor was sufficient to attract those who had previously supported the Democrat party.

Even as small an organization as the National Salvation party had a relatively coherent constituency—namely, reli-

111

giously oriented people and the small shopkeepers in middle Anatolia who felt threatened by the expansion of industrialists and big business. This constituency is now being wooed by the Prosperity party, which scored some success in the municipal elections by taking over a cadre of personalities associated with the banned National Salvation party.

Conversely, when leaders split off from established parties to create their own organizations, the mere presence of an attractive personality at the top does not necessarily compensate for the lack of an established constituency. For example, Turhan Feyzioğlu was not able to impart a distinctive identity to his conservative splinter, despite his personal prominence. Thus politics in Turkey has represented the search for voting blocs to a greater degree than it has represented a leadership popularity contest.

LEADERSHIP

Yet the persistence of patterns from one constitutional period to another does not mean that party leaders are of no or of only small consequence in Turkey. On the contrary, Turks place a high premium on leadership and organizational ability. With the advent of television, oratorical skill is gaining in importance. Thus the phenomenon of an İsmet İnönü, whose commanding position in Turkish politics was not impaired by a speaking voice degraded by deafness, is unlikely to be repeated.

All indications are that Turks want their leaders to appear forceful in command. Looking—as they have customarily done—to the government for a solution to most problems, Turkish voters seem interested in having a sure hand on the tiller. There is even a latent tendency among them to invest political chiefs with the aura of romantic heroes, Atatürk being the most extreme example. But after presiding over the successful military landing on Cyprus, Bülent Ecevit in the 1970s enjoyed something of a cult adulation as a "Second Atatürk" and as the Robin Hood (or Karaoğlan, a Turkish folk hero) of Turkey. Leaders who catch the public imagination thus undoubtedly confer some advantage on their party in the quest for swing votes from the groups at the intersection of the two major constituencies. And Özal's virtuoso performance as a politician who had all the answers clearly helped establish his party rather than the Nationalist Democracy party as the major claimant to represent the right of center.

Without a doubt, the staying power of democratic traditions is also due in part to the quality of leadership in the political arena. It was certainly to the advantage of the Turks that the high status and prestige of government service meant virtually the entire personnel resources of the country were at the disposal of politics. Until recently, business or private careers did not beguile the "best and the brightest." Atatürk, to be sure, may have delayed the advent of multiparty politics through his autocratic behavior and unusually dominant status. But İsmet İnönü's consistent dedication to building democracy as his monument meant that he lent his steady hand and cool eye even in his 80s to help over the rough spots, especially in the difficult transition following the episode of military rule in the early 1960s. Beyond the top leaders, the second- and middle-echelon politicians were often also of substantial ability. There were always many qualified candidates to lead the government as well as phalanxes of choices for the cabinet. "Musical chairs" between a limited pool of ministerial talent has been neither a necessary nor a customary practice in Turkey, where it has been possible to raise up whole new generations of leadership when the previous personalities were excluded from political life. Nor has it been difficult to secure competent administrators or judges to staff the bureaucracy and judiciary.

The present major figures illustrate the ability of the Turkish body politic to regenerate leadership. At the top stands President Kenan Evren, who came to this position through the ratification of the constitution. It was Evren, as ranking general, who had given the order to the armed forces to take power in September 1980; during the period of military rule, he assumed the post of chief of state. A personality of warmth and dignity, he earned considerable popularity as a firm father figure bent on resolving Turkey's ills. Indeed, his popular standing was credited by many for the impressive turnout in the referendum, although subsequent high participation rates in contests in which he played no part suggests that his personality may not have been responsible for that result. President Evren still enjoys high regard; when he speaks, he is generally thought to be voicing the opinions of the military establishment. Despite the continuation of his pushing and hauling with the civilians to define his exact role, his moral authority remains clearly as important as his constitutional powers, which are still to be tested.

The present political party leaders are for the most part latecomers to the national stage. Prime Minister Özal is something of an exception and has a fairly long pedigree in politics. Like Justice party leader Demirel before him, he comes from an engineering background. Indeed, the two worked together in the State Hydraulic Works for a time. Joining the State Planning Organization in 1961, Özal was appointed as its head by Demirel in 1967. After the Justice party government fell before the military ultimatum in 1971, Özal joined the staff of the International Monetary Fund for several years. Having a brother who was a well-connected National Salvation party deputy was also useful in paving the way thereafter to arrange a stint in private enterprise with the large Sabancı Holding Company. When Demirel returned to power at the end of 1979, Özal was made undersecretary in charge of economic affairs and state planning to oversee Turkey's stabilization program in order to make use of his close ties to the international financial community. Özal's strong performance in administering this program won him general admiration; his independence of the military, which first brought him into the cabinet as economic czar and then dismissed him two years later in the wake of a banking scandal, also served him in good stead with the electorate. His emerging talent as a television personality during the campaign in 1983 helped burnish his personal luster as well as that of his party. Although various factions vie for influence in the Motherland party, he stands head and shoulders above the rest in popular esteem and power within the party.

Nonetheless, Özal's leadership style is still evolving. The need to put together in haste a party team to contest elections and then to form a cabinet obliged him to turn to untried personalities, without time to make sure of their compatibility. Initially, he depended on such figures as his brother-in-law, Ali Tanrıyar, who served as minister of the interior. But Özal was unable to make the cabinet operate harmoniously. Thus, after customs officials were arrested for irregularities in policing the Bulgarian border in July 1984, the minister of customs took the floor of parliament in an extraordinary gesture to accuse the minister of the interior of covering up the torture of those detailed in this scandal. With heated controversy on this matter threatening to split the Motherland party and even to deprive Özal of his parliamentary majority, the prime minister relieved both ministers from office in October 1984, amid grumbling over favoritism toward relatives. In December, a deputy from Edirne who was the sister of the dismissed minister of customs resigned from the Motherland party, accusing Özal of autocratic behavior and of having excessively close ties with Muslim fundamentalists. Although this storm was followed in January 1985 with the resignation of Minister of State İsmail Özdağlar, who was charged with receiving bribes, Özal appeared to remain very much in charge of his party. The cycle of action and reaction set in train by these problems did not lead to the exodus of disgruntled elements that the opposition parties were clearly hoping would happen. And Özal was overwhelmingly re-elected Motherland party leader in April 1985 at the party's national convention.

The leadership cadres of the other parties demonstrate how the departure of a generation of party leaders created opportunities for the rise of personalities who might otherwise have remained in the shadow. Erdal İnönü of the Social Democracy party had not heretofore sought to exploit his name recognition as the scion of a politically famous family. During the time that his father was prime minister, he had stayed far from national politics, preferring to become a professor of physics. He was exposed to the vicissitudes of the political process, however, when as rector of the Middle

East Technical University in the turbulent 1970s he was buffeted by left and right extremists. Beyond his distinguished name, it is the presence of other figures with links to the former Republican Peoples party in the top ranks of the new organization that creates in the popular mind the image of the Social Democracy party as the principal left-of-center contender. As his father had done before him, Erdal İnönü displays great political caution. At his party's first national convention, he warned his associates that in the critical period of transition from military to civilian rule, all must walk the narrow line between moderate criticism of the government and extreme opposition that could open his party to charges of obstructionism. The Social Democracy party itself suffers from internal factionalism, although İnönü is clearly the dominant figure in the party. He was reelected party chairman by an overwhelming majority in the party's first national convention in July 1984.

Family connections were also important in the rise of Yildirim Avcı, the initial leader of the True Path party. A medical doctor who started his career in a hospital connected with a state economic enterprise, he served as a physician in Germany during the 1960s and then in a provincial hospital in the Aegean region. After a brief assignment in the Ministry of Health, he was appointed to the Constituent Assembly in 1981. The fact that his brother had been a Justice party deputy from the mid-1960s until he died in the early 1970s was probably instrumental in Avcı's application for the Constituent Assembly. His family's connections with Demirel were clearly responsible for his success in enlisting the cooperation of others who had more or less intimate relationships with the Justice party to join in this venture after the Great Turkey party was closed by the generals for being an open extension of Demirel's party. Avcı's prominence, in fact, derived essentially from his position at the head of the new party, not from his own force of personality or accomplishments. He was thus unable to maintain his leadership of the True Path party as its first national convention approached in May 1985. And he withdrew his candidacy rather than challenge

Hüsamettin Cindoruk who appeared to have Demirel's blessing to take over the True Path party.

Cindoruk had strong credentials as a life-long supporter of the center-right cause. In law school, he had served as chairman of the Democrat party's youth branch in 1952. Although he was temporarily estranged from that party, joining with other dissidents in the Freedom party in 1956, he returned to the Democrat fold after the rebel organization collapsed in the wake of the 1957 elections. He achieved national prominence by service as lawyer for Adnan Menderes in the trials after the 1960 military intervention; he was even jailed briefly for protesting the death sentence imposed on his client. In the 1960s, Cindoruk joined the Justice party. Again he briefly defected from that organization with con-servative leader Sadettin Bilgiç. But Cindoruk soon rejoined Demirel to serve as İstanbul provincial chairman of the Justice party for a few years before the 1980 military takeover. His relationship with Demirel seemed confirmed when the military rulers closed the Great Turkey party which Cindoruk and others had tried to form once political activity was permitted to resume in 1983. And he was one of the handful of politicians sent to Çanakkale with Demirel on the eve of the 1983 elections. Entering the True Path party in 1984, he became its candidate in the party's unsuccessful run for mayor of İstanbul in the March 1984 local elections. His success in besting Union of Chambers of Commerce former president Mehmet Yazar in the True Path party's lower-level congresses leading up to the national convention demonstrated that he was a commanding figure in the party with a charisma and style somewhat reminiscent of those of Demirel himself. And Cindoruk played to the hilt on the theme of restoring rights to "the one who knows" (a widely recognized code phrase for Demirel) without waiting for the expiry of the constitutional ban against party leaders of the Second Republic reentering politics.

Association with the Republican Peoples party was a key ingredient in Necdet Calp's success in forming the Populist party: he had served as private secretary to Prime Minister İsmet İnönü in the 1960s. A career civil servant, his service as secretary to General Gürsel, as chief of state during the 1960–1961 period of military rule, and as undersecretary in the prime ministry up to 1982 evidently earned him the confidence of the military leaders and helped prevent his new party from being excluded from the 1983 elections. Overshadowed by Özal's personality in the election campaign, Calp proved unable to attract centrist votes and was left with no more than the hard core of the left-of-center bloc, which offered no comfortable alternative. Indeed, when broader political competition was permitted in the municipal contests in 1984, the lack of dynamism of the Populist leadership coupled with the wider base of known figures from the past in the Social Democracy party produced a telling decline in Calp's party's appeal. Yet, relying on his parliamentary representation as the major opposition, Calp parried requests to merge with the Social Democracy party. He did keep his election pledge to resign as party president if he ran behind the competition for the allegiance of the left-of-center bloc in the municipal elections. But he was immediately reelected at a miniconvention dominated by the party's elected parliamentarians who were not ready to see the organization break up and thus risk losing their seats.

Retired General Turgut Sunalp owed his position as leader of the Nationalist Democracy party to the sponsorship of the military rulers. Appointed ambassador to Canada after his retirement from active military service in 1970, he had had little experience in partisan politics before beginning to organize his party to woo the center and right-of-center voters. Although he attracted to his organization some of the lower-ranking members of the Justice party and other conservative splinters, he and his associates did not wage an effective campaign in the 1983 parliamentary elections. They could neither forge a credible identity with parties of the previous period of civilian rule, nor could they come forward with a program that seemed significantly different from Özal's recipe. Instead, the Nationalist Democracy party seemed largely content to trade on its reputation as the party of choice of President Evren and his colleagues. As a result, the party ran poorly in November 1983. Accordingly, during the municipal contests the following year, Sunalp's prestige proved unable to stem defections to the emerging True Path party. Like Avcı, Sunalp was reelected to his party post at a miniconvention of his organization's parliamentarians on the heels of this second demonstration of the weakness of the party's popular standing. Indeed, within this party there seemed no alternatives who appeared likely to be able to galvanize support and reverse the fall in popularity.

MOBILIZATION

Although the politicians in Turkey have yet to show any impressive ability to cooperate across party lines, political organizations have operated relatively efficiently to mobilize the voters. Participation in the electoral process has generally been high in national elections, dipping below 60 percent of the eligible voters only in elections in the off years, when the contests were restricted to senatorial competitions in roughly a third of the provinces. Starting from the tradition of universal voting as the duty of citizenry in the one-party era, however, the percentage of those actually going to the polls declined until 1973. Turkey's experience thus ran contrary to the expectations of those who theorize that increasing education, involvement in the political process, and economic development should be accompanied by rising interest in using the ballot. The prevailing explanation of the Turkish performance ascribes the falling rate of participation to the decline in bloc voting as Turkey became more modern. It was argued that as individuals became increasingly responsible for their own voting decisions, there would be a natural decline in the number who would choose to exercise their franchise. The generally higher rate of voter participation during those years in eastern Turkey, where bloc-voting tendencies were and still are most prevalent, was taken as additional confirmation of this hypothesis.

The rebound in the proportion of those voting in 1973 and thereafter, especially in the more developed western provinces, calls this explanation into question. In fact, the process that brought voters back to the polls was a complex one, going far beyond a simple link to modernity and the breakdown of bloc voting.

On the other hand, each military intervention (1960, 1971, and 1980) spurred greater participation in the next immediately following election. The country appeared to be in danger; it was patriotic to vote; and use of the franchise underlined the desire for continuing civilian rule. The departing military rulers themselves encouraged voting as a sign of approval of their new constitutional arrangements. In 1983 they even provided for a financial penalty for those who did not vote. Although the fine was not large, it may also have been an additional inducement in attaining the 92-percent mark, the highest figure ever recorded in multiparty competition in Turkey.

On the other hand, changes in political alignment and the increasing urgency of the issues at stake in the elections, especially after the 1970s, also had a clear impact on the participation rate. The declining proportion of voter turnout in 1965 and 1969 can be linked to a basic political shift that was occurring in those years. The traditional rural notables, who since the founding of the republic had maintained a marriage of convenience with the Republican Peoples party, began to abandon this alliance in 1965 in reaction to that party's newly adopted "left-of-center" election slogans designed to appeal to left-wing voters who might otherwise have slipped over to the Turkish Labor party. The bitter internal dispute attending the exodus of the more conservative faction from Atatürk's party left these rural elements with no natural place to turn. In this situation, these voters appear simply to have stayed home on election day, thus accounting for the sharp drop in the support for their former party as well. By the 1970s, these notables had established a new allegiance to the parties of the right of center; they then returned to the political arena.

By the 1970s, moreover, the national issues facing Turkey appeared particularly acute. In response, the parties in those years ran unusually spirited campaigns, which may well have piqued voter interest to a greater extent than in the past. At the same time, Bülent Ecevit, campaigning as the head of the Republican Peoples party, emerged as a somewhat charismatic figure. His appearances at times galvanized crowds of tens of thousands. In addition, these were years in which radio and television coverage was bringing the election activities more intimately into the lives of Turks throughout the country. Finally, the rapid growth of shantytowns around the major cities also assisted party organizers in increasing the rate of urban participation in election contests.

The confluence of these various factors produced a steady upswing in voting participation from 1973 on. Starting in the urban areas, where recent migrants to the city were exposed to far more intense politicking than would have been possible in a rural setting, this rising tide of interest in using the franchise spread to the more developed provinces of western Turkey. By the 1983 elections, the major urban centers of İstanbul, Ankara, and Adana had been left behind in participation by Thrace, the Aegean provinces, those bordering the Mediterranean, and those on the western and central parts of the Black Sea shore. In fact, except for İstanbul and Ankara, western Turkey universally showed the highest participation rates in the country, scoring above the remarkably high 92-percent national average. The only province in eastern Turkey to do as well was the predominantly Kurdish Bitlis on the western shore of Lake Van. Although that province had been one of those with the highest percentage of voters rejecting the constitution in the referendum, it was the single province in which the Nationalist Democracy party, in winning some 66 percent of the ballots, scored the highest percentage of the vote—the strongest victory margin any party recorded in Turkey in 1983.

PARTY TRENDS

Voter interest in politics is reflected in the dynamism of the party structure. In the First Republic, with elections by majority vote, the victorious party usually (though not invariably) swept the entire slate in a province, no matter what the size of the electoral district. Under these circumstances, the larger parties ended up with the lion's share of the seats;

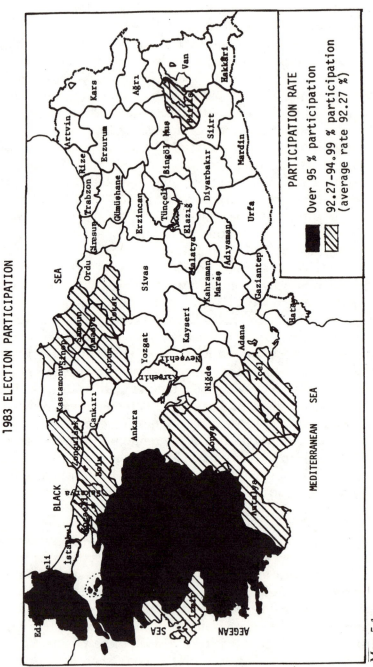

Map 5.1

a minor party had to have a strong base of power in one locality or region in order to be able to elect any deputies at all. For example, the Republican Nation party of Osman Bölükbaşı drew its main strength from his home province of Kırşehir. But it was never able to establish the network of patronage that victory in other provinces would have permitted. Thus it remained a regional organization without any influence on the conduct of government or the composition of the cabinet. In much the same way, efforts by defectors from the Democrat party of Adnan Menderes to establish the Freedom party in 1955 foundered after the insurgents failed to win a single seat except in the tiny province of Burdur, the stronghold of their leader. Recognizing the impossibility of making a major impact on their own, the chiefs of the Freedom party offered to join the Republican Peoples party in 1958. In short, the majority electoral system powerfully discouraged the splintering of the political scene by making it all but impossible for fragments to grow to a size where they could challenge the two major organizations.

The dominance of the two major parties was not as marked in the Second Republic. With the introduction of proportional representation in 1961, the survival of splinter parties was facilitated. In the freer political climate of the ensuing two decades, personality conflicts, coupled with disputes over philosophy and course by rival aspirants to the top positions, contributed to the defection of significant parliamentary factions from the major parties. Turhan Feyzioğlu led his more conservative wing out of the Republican Peoples party in 1967 to found the Reliance party; Sadettin Bilgiç and a group of traditionalists, who were dropped from the cabinet, left the Justice party to form the Democratic party in 1970 (not to be confused with the earlier, and more important, Democrat party of Adnan Menderes). Differences in political outlook also spurred the formation of the National Salvation party, established in 1972 by lower-level defectors from the Justice party to appeal to the traditionalist religious segment of the latter's constituency. These fissiparous tendencies went so far that in 1973 and 1977 neither of the major parties could muster a majority in parliament. Turkey consequently entered its second period of precarious coalition politics, a course that this time led to the downfall of the constitutional system and its replacement, after a few years of military rule, by the Third Republic.

On the strength of these developments, observers both inside and outside of Turkey began to argue that the basically two-party nature of Turkish politics had broken down. Although it was generally recognized that broad left-of-center and right-of-center constituencies still existed, conventional wisdom held that minor parties were becoming solidly entrenched in Turkey's political scene. It was with this fear of political fragmentation that the drafters of the new constitutional order saw it necessary to devise remedies that would limit proportional representation. The imposition of national as well as provincial barriers to disadvantage small parties, the breaking up of the most populous provinces into smaller electoral districts, and the requirement that votes for party candidates be cast for an entire slate were all instituted to encourage the return to an essentially two-party contest.

Yet even as splinter parties were proliferating in response to the attractiveness of the proportional representation system, there were already signs in the 1970s of powerful underlying forces promoting the dominance of two major parties. In fact, a close look at the experience of the small entities that came into being in the Second Republic clearly indicates that the overall record of survival of such minor parties was not impressive. With one exception, these splinter groups all lost support, often dramatically, in every general election after their first appearance on the electoral stage. The New Turkey party, formed in 1961 in an effort to channel supporters of the old regime, faded out entirely after falling from sixty-five seats to six in its third national election. The Turkish Labor party fell from fifteen seats to two in successive elections, although most of this decline was attributable to a change in the voting system to reduce strict proportionality by requiring parties to exceed a provincial rather than a national threshold to quality for seats. After being closed by the military and thus unable to compete in the next election, its electoral support almost disappeared when it was permitted to resume activity and run in 1977. The National Salvation party declined from forty-eight seats in 1973 to twenty-four in 1977, whereas the Democratic party and Republican Reliance party were nearly wiped out in 1977.

Only the extreme right-wing Nationalist Action party managed to buck this trend, rising from one seat in the lower house in 1969 to sixteen in 1977. Its new lease on life came after it was taken over by Alparslan Turkeş, a protofascist. His participation in the coalition government of the day was thought to have added legitimacy to his extreme approach; many observers in Turkey believed that the party was continuing to gain momentum when the military stepped in to end political activity and jail Turkeş. Yet its gains did not offset the losses of the other minor parties. And although the splinter parties from 1973 to 1980 occupied a swing position between the relatively evenly matched majors, their total bulk was receding significantly by the end of the period.

The experience of the Third Republic is too short to derive conclusive evidence of the continuation of the trend toward two-party dominance. Nonetheless, the performance of the various parties in the parliamentary elections of 1983 and the countrywide mayoral-provincial assembly elections of 1984 suggests that a shaking-out process is under way. The next elections are likely to see further consolidation of the larger entities, whereas several of the smaller ones seem destined not to be able to cross the 10-percent national barrier. Indeed, this prospect may lead to mergers between like-minded parties. There has already been some exploration of the possibility that the Populist party might join with the Social Democracy party. Similarly, there is continuing pressure on the Nationalist Democracy party to fold itself into the True Path party to escape complete electoral defeat. The Prosperity party is so small that it will be hard put to qualify for any seats in the general elections as well. Indeed, either before or after the coming elections, the number of serious contenders on the political scene is likely to diminish rather than to grow, even if one or two additional minor parties come onto the scene.

The fact that splinter groups have generally shown little

staying power relates to a number of factors. Their survival depends directly on the nature of the electoral system: the further from full proportional representation, the less encouraging to smaller parties. Even when electoral provisions have been relatively favorable, a number of psychological pressures against minor parties exist. Turks, like most peoples, value strong national leadership. Indeed, given the depth of emotional attachment of most Turks to patriotism and the welfare of their country, the yearning for a decisive hand in charge is quite understandable. Especially in this era, when Turkey faces difficult economic and social problems, the value of a commanding personality at the head of an effective government is readily apparent. There is a general desire to avoid drift in Turkey. In this connection, most Turkish voters seem to recognize that only by backing a major party can the requisite leadership be found. The electorate seems largely convinced that a ballot for a minor party can be merely a means of protest, but that for effective action one must opt for one of the serious contenders for power. Such a bandwagon effect strongly favors the larger entities. It is the largest parties, moreover, that have the greatest reserves of impressive talent; the splinter groups generally have only one or two well-known figures. And finally, the inability of many minor parties to carve out a well-defined constituency prevents them from growing and makes their survival difficult.

LOCALISM

Turkish parties reflect institutionalized tensions between national and local interests. In Turkey, reformist politics have always been national; local interests, on the other hand, have continually been opposed to far-reaching social and cultural reform. The accommodation of these conflicting points of view, while preserving the essence of Atatürk's pragmatic modernizing thrust, has been one of the major achievements of Turkey's political life. Thus the political contest has focused especially on tactics to achieve development and on the issue of how much disruption of traditional social mores is necessary for advance. But Turkey's general direction and broad societal goals have achieved a wide, though not unanimous, consensus.

In the one-party era, little moment was attached to local desires with respect to representation in the assembly. Deputies were assigned to provinces without regard to their ties to those localities. Indeed, throughout its existence, the top leadership of the Republican Peoples party was singularly unconcerned about identification with a particular locality of origin. Atatürk, after all, was born in Salonika, a place not even within the bounds of modern Turkey. Although originally from İzmir and brought up in Sivas, İsmet İnönü did have family associations with Malatya, which eventually became his electoral constituency; he maintained his home in Ankara and in İstanbul, however—not in Malatya. Despite the fact the Bülent Ecevit was a native of İstanbul, he never represented this constituency; he ran from Ankara before shifting to Zonguldak in 1965 to emphasize his solidarity with workers in the mines and mills of this labor center.

This bias against localism on the part of national politicians is enshrined in the constitution, which, from the start of the republic, has provided that deputies represent not their local districts but the nation as a whole. Thus, in all of the larger parties, none of which is regionally based, some of the more prominent figures run in electoral districts with which they are not intimately associated. For example, Motherland party leader Özal was born in Malatya and was elected from İstanbul. Nonetheless, this party was more locally oriented than its rivals; a higher percentage of its deputies represented strong local ties than did the deputies of the other parties. The Nationalist Democracy party displayed the most extreme disdain for local sensitivities. About 20 percent of its elected deputies were born outside of the provinces in which they ran and were put at the head of the list in large, hence safer, constituencies. In the main, these were older candidates who had established reputations in politics, the bureaucracy, and military service. Overall, in almost every large province some of the current deputies are not natives of their electoral district.

Nonetheless, although party, not personality, still remains

the key to electoral success in the more developed regions of Turkey, the multiparty era stimulated greater concern with selecting candidates who were popular in their electoral districts. Justice party leader Demirel was the first major party leader to eschew the safety of a large province to run in his hometown—in this case, İsparta. Voters in Turkey, as in most polities, when they have the choice, seem to prefer to be represented by fellow natives rather than by outsiders—at least unless the latter are of uncommon national or international stature. Hence the Democrat party sought to emphasize its democratic nature as early as 1949 by prohibiting the national headquarters from putting nominees in more than 20 percent of the places on local provincial slates. The Republican Peoples party also moved in this direction, even though its leadership retained the right to name 30 percent of the party's candidates in the 1950s.

Legal restrictions on the ability of the party headquarters to place candidates on the local lists were imposed in the election laws of the Second and Third Republics. But while these statutes limited the national leadership to controlling only 5 percent of the party's slate, candidate selection has always occasioned controversy. In the 1977 elections, for example, the placing of figures not native to the province at the head of the local tickets perceptibly affected the results in a number of smaller provinces. In other cases, especially in eastern Turkey, the failure of aspirants with strong local bases to win the desired place on the lists led them to abandon the party altogether after the primaries and to run on their own as independents. In fact, the four successfully elected independents in 1977 had all quit major parties when denied choice spots on the party tickets. It was with this baleful example in mind that the right of popular local figures to keep their positions at the head of the list was provided in the current election law.

In this situation, politics in Turkey has assumed a character progressively more responsive to local issues and interests. One of the principal ways in which localism has modified Turkey's course is seen in the realm of policy toward Islam. Atatürk was personally irreligious and, like many reformers of his generation, saw attachment to religion as the main impediment to westernizing Turkey. He therefore disestablished Islam as the state religion and imposed rigorous discrimination against its practice. He closed the dervish lay religious orders, which had formed a separate hierarchy outside the control and guidance of the orthodox religious establishment—an establishment that, itself, had been a wing of the government. The formal orthodoxy was also restricted. Religious schools of all sorts were closed, and clerics were prohibited from circulating in religious garb except in places of worship. Turkish was imposed in place of Arabic as the language of worship. In short, the full weight of the government was directed at discouraging the observance of religion.

Multiparty competition itself worked to relax these restrictions. To woo voters, optional courses on religion were added to the curriculum in the 1940s; a faculty of divinity was reopened; Arabic was restored in religious services; and a proliferation of local training schools for worship leaders was eventually permitted. Moreover, as local interests grew stronger and the reformist leadership of the major parties became comparatively weaker, the public observance of religious festivals increased. A binge of mosque building began, capped by the construction of a huge and prominent structure dominating the skyline of new Ankara—a development inconceivable in Atatürk's lifetime. By the 1970s, it had become fashionable for government officials to fast during Ramadan; many educated people could be seen at Friday noon prayers, even before the rise of the National Salvation party, which frankly catered to and encouraged this development.

These trends toward a resurgence of religious observance have gained sufficient momentum that even the strongly secular Atatürk-style reformist bent of the generals after 1980 did not seriously set back the public exercise of religious practice. Özal himself is religiously observant, and his evident piety seems to have served as something of a vote getter for his party. Critics have claimed that elements in the Motherland party coming from a National Salvation party background enjoyed particular favor and access to important posts. The

Motherland party administration's dictum on greater conservatism in dress in the May 19 athletic celebrations in 1984 added to the impression that religious custom would be more respected than in the past. And charges were leveled at the Özal government that its politicians gave an additional fillip to social pressures to attend the mosque.

RISE OF NEW GROUPS

Localism has also fostered changes in the socioeconomic interests represented in parliament. Over the years, the constant current toward broadening the social strata represented in the assembly has been only temporarily diverted by the ebb and flow of military interventions into politics. Atatürk's successful revolt against the sultan was accompanied by a marked influx of comrades at arms into the political arena. Former high-ranking officers were brought into parliament in droves; they staffed important posts in the cabinet and participated in key parliamentary committees in the early years of the First Republic. But as the revolution matured, their numbers diminished in favor of lawyers in particular—the category of politicians that forms a sizable proportion of civilian parliamentarians throughout the world. Doctors and other professionals also increased in their representation, even before the transition to multiparty politics toward the end of the First Republic. Businessmen, as well, rose in numbers as the political contest broadened with the end of the one-party era. That process imparted to the assembly an outlook considerably different from the government-oriented, reformist elite approach pursued at the start of this period.

The trend toward increasing business and professional representation in political life continued in the 1960s and 1970s, interrupted only by the mild comeback of retired officers in the initial parliament following the military rule in 1960–1961. In subsequent elections, the numbers of former members of the armed forces declined again until they formed only about 3 percent of the membership of the lower house in 1980 on the eve of the latest military intervention. By contrast, the contingent of farmers was over twice as large

as that of retired officers in the final assembly of the Second
Republic. Those involved with religious affairs, a category
that had been steadily reduced during the First Republic,
increased during the 1970s and ended that decade with 4
percent of the members of the lower house claiming that
affiliation under the impress of the rise of the National
Salvation party. Engineers were also expanding their representation in the assembly; by the end of the Second Republic,
8 percent of the deputies had been trained in that profession.
Economists, too, emerged as a significant bloc, holding some
5 percent of the seats in the lower house by 1980. Yet lawyers
came to constitute by far the most populous group in the
assembly, numbering over one-fourth of the deputies. Even
though the rough and tumble of party competition decreased
the continuity of membership in the assembly as compared
with the situation in the First Republic (except for the major
shift in membership in 1950, when the opposition Democrat
party ousted the Republican Peoples party), for most elections
in the Second Republic, half of the deputies regularly had
some prior parliamentary experience. This continuity ensured
that the trends in the evolution of parliamentary membership
would be largely unaffected by the otherwise radical changes
introduced by the military regime in 1960–1961.

As in the past, the military takeover in 1980 raised the
visibility of retired officers on the political scene. But many
who ran as candidates on the Nationalist Democracy party
ticket failed to be elected. Thus, while former military officers
more than doubled their proportion in the 1983 parliament
over that in 1980, those with a military background (25 out
of the 400-seat assembly) played a relatively minor role in
the leadership of the new parliament. None served in the
cabinet, and their presence was far less significant than that
of some other groups.

Much more influential in terms of power and policy was
the new complexion provided by the probusiness orientation
of the Motherland party. Trained as an engineer, Turgut Özal
drew on a large contingent of individuals with similar back-
grounds to form his party. Indeed, engineers and contractors
formed the largest professional category in the assembly that

took office in 1983. The number of public administrators, another group with which Özal shared intimate connections in the past, also rose dramatically. By contrast, lawyers, farmers, those involved in religious affairs, and dentists suffered significant declines in numbers. In part, their loss of representation reflected objections by the generals, who used their constitutional authority to veto the candidacies of all who had close ties to the parties of the Second Republic. Likewise, the military rulers screened out elements they considered insufficiently attached to the secular principles of Kemalism. They also vetoed the candidacies of 101 former parliamentarians who had sought to run on party tickets and particularly as independents in the November 1983 race. As a result, the assembly elected in 1983 had only a small number of members who had ever served before in parliament: only seven individuals had been previously elected to the deputy level more than twice. This lack of parliamentary experience contributed a certain hesitancy and tentativeness to the initial operations of the 1983 assembly.

Whereas it might been expected that the removal of a generation of entrenched politicians would have opened the way for the rise of younger people as deputies, the new assembly proved to be populated with somewhat older figures than before. To be sure, the Motherland party deputies, on the average, were approximately the same age at election as were the members of the last civilian parliament of the Second Republic. Populist and Nationalist Democracy representatives averaged some five and ten years older, respectively, than the previous norm for elected representatives. Deputies from urban constituencies, irrespective of party, proved to be significantly older than were those drawn from more rural districts, thus indicating that where tribal and other primordial ties were weakest, age remained a prime characteristic of status of prestige. Indeed, this outcome provides an additional indicator that for all the electoral engineering of the Third Republic, the new system had not basically changed the mechanisms on which electoral appeal was based in Turkey.

The entry into politics of men and women from new economic strata had its effect on deliberations concerning domestic policy above all. The question of economic approach, the role of central planning, and the proper place for private enterprise were debated with growing intensity as the new arrivals challenged the older notion of state-directed reform. Clustered around first the Democrat party, later the Justice party, and now the Motherland and True Path parties, these elements with their nongovernmental focus have been attacked as seeking to dismantle the etatist economic structure. In fact, the dispute has been more a question of emphasis than one of principle. Even the new people accept a heavy state involvement. Although the Motherland party is seeking ways to sell to private ownership a share in some of the profit-making state economic enterprises, Özal has no thought of turning over those that provide essential public services.

Just as the rise of the right-of-center constituency has been attributed to the burgeoning of the middle class, some Turkish scholars have judged the recent emergence of a sizable industrial labor force as a development favoring the left-of-center bloc. The rebound of the Republican Peoples party from its low point in 1969 fueled this interpretation. From just over 27 percent of the votes in that year, the party of Atatürk managed to rise to over 41 percent in the 1977 elections. Historically, the Republican Peoples party was the party of the educated elite in Turkey. A bias toward it and its reformist approach was built into the educational system, despite the efforts of the Justice party and especially the National Salvation party to uproot that bias. As Turkey developed, therefore, and as migration to the cities brings more youth within easy reach of at least primary educational institutions, the reformist approach was expected by these Turkish scholars to gain significant new adherents.

Based on Turkey's experience in the 1970s, some investigators even put forth the hypothesis that Turkish development had proceeded to the point of producing a "critical realignment" of voter support—a revolution in attitude away from "territorial and cultural cleavages" and toward voting along class lines. Protagonists of this view asserted that such a realignment accounted for the gains scored by the Republican Peoples party in the last two general elections of the Second

Republic. That party's socialist approach gave it claims to represent the interests of the workers and fast-growing urban areas.

Although this theory was comforting to the Turkish elite in promising that its favored party would dominate the political scene in the future, it appears to contain a large dose of wishful thinking. As yet there is no convincing evidence that sectional, ethnic, linguistic, religious, and cultural factors have weakened in their saliency in affecting voting patterns in developed pluralistic societies, let alone in developing polities where traditional values bulk larger. Why the Turks should be more prone to functional solidarity than peoples elsewhere is not readily apparent; indeed, such a belief flies in the face of more recent experience in Turkey.

The improvement in the fortunes of the Republican Peoples party in the 1970s was encouraged in large part by psychological factors unrelated to economic development or social change. First was the shock that the Justice party suffered in its confrontation with the military in the "Coup by Memorandum" in 1971. In the ensuing election Demirel was at a distinct disadvantage in projecting the image of one who could govern effectively. His campaign thus lacked the spirit and fire characteristic of his performances in the 1960s. This loss of confidence clearly discouraged his normal constituency, which was further fractured by the defections of the Democratic party and the National Salvation party at this time. But a look at the combined percentage of the vote received by the right-of-center parties in elections in the Second Republic (see Table 5.1) clearly shows the impressive consistency of the vote for this total constituency, with no clear trend toward the left-of-center alignment.

In 1977, although Demirel ran a considerably more confident campaign, having returned to office as prime minister, he faced Ecevit, who had emerged in the interval as something of a popular hero. Ecevit's appeal was based on his oratorical ability to project a populist aura, coupled with the remnants of the national exaltation he had earned from ordering the intervention in Cyprus in 1974. Fears among his party's normal constituency that his "left-of-center" slogan was synonymous with communism had by this time long since died out, as had the memories of his party's high-handedness during the one-party era. In this more favorable atmosphere, his campaign style unquestionably impressed the voters, who turned out in large crowds to hear him. Yet, as the statistics show, he was largely preaching to the converted until 1977, when the urgency of Turkey's problems led the center to seek the decisive leadership that his candidacy then suggested.

But Ecevit's ability to profit from national euphoria did not last. When his coalition government proved unable either to contain political violence and terrorism or to cope with the pressing economic problems of the day, the popularity of the Republican Peoples party dropped precipitously. In the senatorial elections in 1979, in one-third of Turkey's provinces, Ecevit's party declined from the 42 percent of the vote it had garnered two years previously. With only 29 percent of the vote in 1979, the Republican Peoples party ran far behind the Justice party, which had boosted its total from the 38 percent in 1977 to nearly 47 percent two years later. The sharpness of the decline of left-of-center support led Ecevit to abandon efforts to remain at the head of government. It also demonstrated clearly that voters in Turkey do not cast their ballots on a class basis.

Rather than a "critical realignment," therefore, the ups and downs of the fortunes of the major parties in Turkey appear to reflect the fact that Turkish politics is essentially a struggle between the ins and the outs. The desire to change the party in office seems to grow in Turkey after two general elections in power. The Democrat party would have lost the 1957 elections had it not changed the election rules on the eve of these contests. Similarly, the Justice party suffered a sharp reverse in the 1970s after winning with impressive margins in the 1960s. Finally, the Republican Peoples party's string appeared to be running out at the end of the 1970s, when it, too, failed to show the voters that it could keep the promises it had made when it came to power. Although experience in the Third Republic has been far too short to

TABLE 5.1 Election Results in the Second and Third Republics: 1961–1984 (in percentages)

Years	Second Republic 450-member lower house					Third Republic		
	1961	1965	1969	1973	1977	400-member national assembly 1983	Mayoral election 1984	Provincial Assembly 1984
Participation rates	81.0	71.3	64.3	66.8	72.5	92.3	85.6	91.0
Left-of-Center Totals	36.7	31.7	32.9	34.3	41.9	30.5	32.6	32.2
Republican Peoples party	36.7	28.7	27.4	33.2	41.4			
Turkish Unity Party			2.8	1.1	.4			
Turkish Labor party		3.0	2.7	closed	.1			
Populist party						30.5	7.8	8.8
Social Democracy party							24.8	23.4

TABLE 5.1 (continued)

Right-of-Center Totals	62.5	65.1	61.5	62.8	55.6	68.5	64.3	66.9
Justice party	34.8	52.9	46.5	29.8	36.9			
National Salvation party				11.9	8.6			
Nationalist Action party	14.0	2.2	3.0	3.4	6.4			
Republican Reliance party			6.6	5.3	1.9			
Democratic Party				11.8	1.8			
New Turkey party	13.7	3.7	2.2					
Nation party		6.3	3.2	.6				
Motherland party						45.2	43.2	41.5
Nationalist Democracy party						23.3	5.4	7.0
True Path party							11.9	14.0
Prosperity party							3.8	4.4
Independents Totals	.8	3.2	5.6	2.8	2.5	1.1	3.2	1.6

TABLE 5.2 Election Results in the Second and Third Republics: 1961–1984 (in seats)

| | Second Republic | | | | | Third Republic | | |
| | 450-member lower house | | | | | 400-member national assembly | Mayoral election | Provincial Assembly |
Years	1961	1965	1969	1973	1977	1983	1984	1984
Left-of-Center Totals	173	149	153	186	213	117	378	564
Republican Peoples party	173	134	143	185	213			
Turkish Unity Party			8	1				
Turkish Labor party		15	2					
Populist party						117	94	58
Social Democracy party							284	506

TABLE 5.2 (continued)

Right-of-Center Totals	277	301	284	258	233	282	1,243	1,721
Justice party	158	240	256	149	189		883	
National Salvation party				48	24			
Nationalist Action party	54	11	1	3	16			
Republican Reliance party			15	13	3			
Democratic party				45	1			
New Turkey party	65	19	6					
Nation party		31	6					
Motherland party						211	883	1,420
Nationalist Democracy party						71	106	99
True Path party							238	188
Prosperity party							16	14
Independents Totals			13	6	4		80	21

TABLE 5.3 Election Results in the Second Republic: The Senate

	1961	1964	1966	1968	1973	1975	1977	1979
Participation Rates	*81.4%	60.2%	56.2%	66.3%	*65.3%	58.4%	*73.8%	70.6%
Left-of-Center Totals	37.2%	40.8%	33.9%	31.8%	35.7%	44.3%	42.3%	33.0%
Republican Peoples party	37.2%	40.8%	30.0%	27.1%	33.6%	43.8%	42.3%	29.1%
Turkish Unity party					2.1%	.5%		1.2%
Turkish Labor party			3.9%	4.7%				.7%
Socialist Workers party of Turkey								1.3%
Socialist Revolutionary party								.7%
Right-of-Center Totals	63.0%	56.5%	66.4%	66.5%	62.3%	55.9%	57.6%	65.6%
Justice party	35.5%	50.3%	56.3%	49.9%	31.0%	40.8%	38.3%	46.8%
National Salvation party					12.3%	8.8%	8.4%	9.7%
Democratic party					10.4%	3.1%	2.2%	
National Action party	13.5%	3.0%	1.9%	2.0%	2.7%	3.2%	6.8%	6.6%
New Turkey party	14.0%	3.5%	2.3%					
Nation party			5.9%	6.0%				
Republican Reliance party				8.6%	5.9%		1.9%	2.5%
Independents Totals	.3%	2.3%	.5%	1.7%	2.0%	.1%		1.3%

*coincided with general elections to the lower house

tell whether a rough two-term limit on retaining popularity
will continue, there is no reason to doubt that it is the ability
of the ruling party to govern effectively and find solutions
to major problems that will ultimately determine its staying
power.

THE CHALLENGE OF TERRORISM

A dynamic factor severely testing the Turkish system
has been the evolution of terrorism. Why political violence
should have flourished in the 1960s and especially in the
1970s, given its relative absence in the 1940s and 1950s, still
defies a complete explanation. That makes it tempting to
ascribe Turkey's descent into violence to underlying processes
of social dislocation as the population became increasingly
mobile and entered the modernized sector of life. Indeed,
there is much to recommend the attribution of the rise of
terrorism as a political force to the breakdown of customary
social mechanisms of control. Yet that is by no means the
whole story, even as far as it can be discerned from the
present inadequate evidence. The process of the breakdown
of respect for authority among fringe groups clearly resulted
from a complex interaction of many elements.

The inculcation of respect for the state, its law, and its
coercive apparatus was a cardinal goal of Atatürk's Turkey.
Under the one-party regime, dissent was identified with
disloyalty to the republic and was put down before it could
spread. On the other hand, patriotism was extolled as the
supreme civic virtue. Disorder did accompany the transition
to multiparty politics in the latter 1940s, but the trouble then
stemmed mostly from the inability of the security forces to
adapt to the need to tolerate the organization of a legitimate
political opposition. What little violence there was in the early
1950s was evidenced mainly in the attempted assassination
of a prominent liberal journalist by a religious reactionary in
1952. That incident indicated that it was the conservatives
who took advantage of the relative relaxation of constraints
after the victory of the Democrat party, whereas there was
no letup in pressure on the left. The aura of foreign danger

from the Soviets starting in 1945 made repression of the left seem a patriotic action; hence there was little overt resistance to government efforts to crack down on those few who raised their heads.

By the end of the 1950s, however, the picture had changed. Democrat party efforts to restrict the freedom of speech of İsmet İnönü and his Republican Peoples party in 1959 by rock-throwing toughs who sought to disrupt his Aegean speaking tour generated popular defiance of the authorities. Rumors of police brutality touched off student protests, which the police attempted to disperse with gunfire. When the Democrats had recourse to martial law in an effort to reimpose order, even the students at the military academy demonstrated against the government, marching on the Presidential Palace. This boldness of the young in challenging the government influenced the thinking both of politicians, who became reluctant to repress student outbursts for fear of provoking a military response, and of youth, who saw open defiance of authority as an effective and legitimate political tool. Nevertheless, with the military takeover of 1960, the impetus for violent protest ebbed among the young. The campuses quickly returned to calm.

The upsurge of political violence in the 1960s still cannot be completely explained. One factor in the process was no doubt the efforts of rightists to disrupt the emerging Turkish Labor party, which came into being after the junta restored political activity in 1961. Turkish Labor party rallies were natural targets for rightists who had cut their teeth on government-sponsored demonstrations against the left in the mid-1940s. This pattern of forceful confrontation was repeated in the universities, where, in the expanded freedom of the 1960s, socialism became the vogue for a majority of the students. Violent fights between hotheads representing both poles of view became common on campuses. The hostility spread to the labor movement when leftist unionists challenged the more conservative confederation of labor for domination of individual unions.

It was out of this charged atmosphere of physical violence that clandestine groups of political terrorists evolved. It is nonetheless unclear as to how the unplanned visceral hostility of left and right blossomed into a deliberate campaign against law and order. Part of the answer seems to lie in the inclination of leftist students to reduce doctrine to action and to take up anarchist philosophies. Also significant was the impact of Palestinian terrorism in the aftermath of the 1967 war in the Middle East, for a number of Turkish youths gravitated to Palestinian training camps to learn the skills of terror as a political weapon at this time. Thus terror as a tool to work against the regime was associated in the late 1960s with extreme-left fragments that had gone beyond Soviet-style doctrines and were following such inspirations as those of Carlos Marighella, the prophet of the urban guerrillas in Latin America. To publicize their cause, these extremist groups began kidnappings of U.S. military personnel in Turkey, in the process also embarrassing the government and drawing attention to its relationship with the United States. In addition, they perpetrated the killings of Turks and were responsible for the kidnap-murder of the Israeli consul general in İstanbul.

This era of sensationalist terrorist acts ended with the 1971 military intervention. The terrorism of the 1960s was punctuated by a few spectacular incidents against a backdrop of campus violence; most of the rest of Turkish life was unaffected by terrorism. Yet the disruption of institutions of higher learning, as student terrorists took advantage of the university autonomy that provided a measure of immunity from police searches without the permission of the rector, boded ill for hopes of depoliticizing the educational system.

Energetically applied martial law quickly suppressed the political violence. But while the jailing of many suspects ended disorder, the prison experience may have turned some sympathizers into hard-core activists. The execution of some young figures created heroes, such as Deniz Gezmiş and Mahir Çayan, who appealed to fellow youths who were seeking freedom from society's restrictions. This period of enforced quiescence under martial law laid the base for further fragmentation of the extreme left into competing units. It also sent surviving cells deep underground, giving them both the experience and the motivation to resume activity when possible.

Amnesty in 1974 for those jailed for fomenting disorder was followed by a significant upsurge of violence. Part of the cause for the return to political activism may have been the frustration that leftist parties felt at being excluded from the 1973 voting. The notion of an "out-of-parliament opposition" that therefore had no alternative to operating outside the system became popular in leftist circles in the aftermath of these contests. But a major part of the reason for renewed challenge to the regime at this time appears to have been the return of those jailed. This signified that the government would no longer take draconian measures against political extremists, a conclusion that was only reinforced by the growing political ineffectiveness of coalition politics.

The political violence of the latter 1970s, however, differed greatly from that of the 1960s in several important respects. First, some of the new disorder was essentially communal conflict, in which one social group expressed its deep antipathy against others who differed in religious sect, place of origin, or political outlook. That was the mechanism involved in the sensational Kahramanmaraş incident, for instance, but it was also behind many other small-scale disturbances in which one squatter community battled with its neighbor. At bottom, this violence appears to have reflected the import of traditional rural score-settling methods to an urban setting.

Second, some of the disorder resulted from local politicians attempting to defy the authorities by setting up so-called liberated zones, in which the normal legal writ of the country was rejected. Such open defiance—the most notable instance being the "liberation" of Fatsa township of Ordu province, which the army eventually had to quell—probably derived from the conviction that the central government would be unable to act. Whatever the causes, this open rejection of authority was new in kind from the incidents in the 1960s.

A third major difference from the norms of the earlier period was the addition of ethnic violence to the mix. By the late 1970s, Kurdish clandestine groups had been organized, some of which claimed to be promoting separatism. Not all of these groups asserting such claims were sincere; some sought an aura that might legitimize bandit acts in the eyes of the local population in rural tribal areas. In İstanbul and other urban centers, Kurds seemed associated with ethnic Turks in the terrorist movement. In these organizations, a better deal for the Kurds was only one of the aims of the violence.

Overall, the most striking difference between the activities of the earlier period as compared with the later lay in the spread and persistence of terror. After 1975, incidents fed on incidents. And the common perception that the government lacked the will to impose order seemed an open invitation to political terrorism, which mounted rapidly in the last years of the Second Republic. The welcoming environment for violence was especially instrumental in promoting terrorism by the right, for by no means were all of the perpetrators of terror leftists or anarchists. The Commandos of the Nationalist Action party traded on government tolerance to organize and inflict violence on the left whenever the opportunity arose. With cabinets depending on support from the Nationalist Action party, it was clearly difficult for the security forces to act decisively against the Commandos.

The question of the significance and degree of foreign involvement in the Turkish terrorist movement cannot be resolved on present evidence. Communist propaganda in the 1970s called the Turkish people to vote for the left-of-center Republican Peoples party rather than for the Turkish Labor party, which had no realistic chance of election. The implication is that the Soviets did not believe that an all-out challenge to the regime by domestic forces could succeed. Moreover, the terrorists in Turkey were not all well disposed toward the Soviet Union: Maoists, Trotskyists, and anarchists expressed degrees of hostility to Moscow. Turkish authorities and some foreign observers have nonetheless seen a foreign hand stirring up violence to weaken the regime in Turkey. They also point to the huge arsenal of weapons recovered by the security forces to back up their argument that such quantities demonstrate foreign provenance. But however much foreign agitation and money may have been in evidence, the main causative factors seem likely to have been domestic in nature.

Firm action by the generals quickly restored order after the commanders seized the reins of government in 1980. Massive arrests swept up those who were involved in terrorism, as well as those who may have been only sympathetic to this cause. But with continuing encouragement from Turks in Germany, which served as a sort of safehaven, would-be terrorists persisted in plotting. The security forces made periodic arrests of armed elements, almost always before the conspirators could actually launch their actions. But it was clear that while martial law was effective in blunting terrorism, all the impetus for using violence as a political weapon had not been removed from the system.

Thus Turkey returned to party competition in 1983 without having completely eliminated terrorism. Even during the first year under civilian hands, efforts to promote various forms of violence continued, though generally without marked success. The boldest challenge came from the Kurdish separatists, who launched several widely scattered attacks on gendarmerie posts in eastern Turkey. That was an argument for slowness in removing martial law, although the politicians evinced some confidence that indigenous fringe groups would not again be able to disrupt the political scene. Nonetheless, in the background many questions remained about how to treat the thousands in jail and awaiting trial, given that, except for demonstrating a continuing firm hand, the government had not basically changed the environment.

THE DYNAMICS OF HUMAN RIGHTS

Violence also brought to the fore a perennial political issue for Turkey: the quest for human rights. The struggle to entrench and expand respect for the elemental rights of citizens had been woven into the fabric of the Ottoman reform effort. Abolition of the Janissary slave troops and the end of the process of slave recruitment in the nineteenth century testified to a basic advance in human rights as all citizens gained in independence to pursue their livelihoods. Starting from the Tanzimat, equality before the law was enunciated as a theoretical construct, although to the last days of the empire this precept was only slowly and imperfectly applied as a guide for government conduct toward citizens. The introduction of Western law codes by Atatürk carried the process further, but it still did not bring Turkish compliance up to European standards.

The course toward the freer exercise of human rights has had to contend with powerful obstacles in Turkish society. Part of the problem stems from the difficulties in grafting alien legal concepts onto a traditional social system in which the ruling class had been exempt from many of the obligations incumbent on the common citizen. Thus, for example, the police, who were drawn from the lower strata of society, found it nearly impossible to gain the respect of the upper classes and treated members of the elite with deference even when the latter had committed clear infractions of the law. On the other hand, the security forces felt little compulsion to be sensitive to the rights of the masses; when an ordinary citizen fell into the hands of the police even in republican Turkey, he was often dealt with harshly. Indeed, one of the issues exploited most tellingly against the Republican Peoples party in the late 1940s by the Democrat party was the frequent brutality of the gendarmerie toward the rural populace. Once in power, the Democrats in turn were widely accused in the 1950s of using the police to manhandle students; these charges so undermined police authority that the Democrat party had to turn to the army to keep order in 1960, thus sealing the course toward revolution.

The tradition of strong government controls over the citizenry also impeded the progress of winning human rights. Even such practices as restricting movement and the involuntary settling of population groups remained alive in the Turkish Republic. From the earliest days of the Ottoman Empire, the sultans had transported unruly or potentially difficult subjects to the frontiers. The settlement of tribes in the nineteenth century continued this pattern of government intrusion into living arrangements. Abdül Hamid II imposed a ban on settlements in the Holy Land by Jewish immigrants from czarist domains toward the turn of the twentieth century. His successors' efforts to transport Armenians from border areas with Russia during World War I occasioned great loss of life and aroused the undying hostility of Armenians toward Turks. In a more positive vein, Atatürk followed the trend of population engineering by arranging large-scale exchanges of ethnic groups with Greece and Bulgaria. He also sought to ensure tranquillity in his eastern provinces by removing restive Kurdish tribal leaders to enforced residence elsewhere. This precedent was repeated after the 1960 military intervention, when fifty-five Kurdish notables were resettled outside their tribal areas during the interlude of military rule. And again in 1984, at a time when raids on police posts in the Kurdish areas of Turkey provoked an extensive security sweep in the Turkish provinces bordering Iraq, the central government apparently moved some of the populace out of the region.[1]

Another barrier to achieving human rights in Turkey was the long tradition of censorship and restrictions on the freedom of expression. The press from its start in Ottoman days was under the heavy thumb of government; indeed, the earliest serial publication venture in the Turkish language represented essentially a report of government activity. Abdül Hamid II exercised pervasive censorship over the private press organs that proliferated inside Turkey in the latter years of the nineteenth century. Freedom of the press, enjoyed only briefly in the Young Turk era, became a constant element of dispute in the political controversies of republican Turkey. The extreme left advanced the demand for an unrestricted press as one of its central goals following the closure of Communist party organs in 1925. And after World War II, leftists took advantage of a brief relaxation of controls to publish actively, leading the government to crack down. Efforts by the religious right to engage in circulating underground tracts, once it had recovered from the initial assaults of Kemalist reform, fed into the competition for votes as Turkey moved into multiparty politics after Atatürk's death. But severe press laws and retaliation against publications espousing unpopular views or criticizing the authorities remained a standard weapon in the government's armory.

These various strands of the unfinished course of achieving fuller human rights in Turkey came together in the Second Republic, which was a time of great personal freedom. At the extremes, communist literature was openly printed and distributed in Turkey for the first time since 1925, and the religious right took advantage of the permissive climate to spread its message. This heady atmosphere was interrupted briefly by the two years of military-backed above-party governments following the ultimatum of 1971. But by the end of the 1970s, the scope for political activity had broadened to the point where the question of legalizing the Communist party was being given serious consideration by the major parties. Freedom of expression confronted few bounds.

This heyday of political and civil rights was brought to an abrupt end by the military takeover of 1980. It was the conclusion of important groups in Turkey, especially the armed forces, that excess license and indiscipline in society bore a major share of the responsibility for the disruption of normal governmental process in Turkey. Valuing the welfare of society above the rights of individuals, the generals saw the need to prevent anarchy—at whatever cost to personal rights that might be necessary. They thus swept up large numbers of suspects charged with terrorism, with espousing illegal political doctrines, and with seeking to divide the state. In narrowing the legal political arena to exclude the extremes of left and right, the generals applied a heavy hand to the press and restricted politicians from the old regime.

The incarceration of tens of thousands, mostly young people, charged with or suspected of violating the basic code of democratic conduct and the sanctity of the state, created an environment in which emotions ran high. Hostility toward prisoners by their jailers was difficult to control. Not surprising, therefore, were the number of incidents involving physical mistreatment of detainees. Yet torture was clearly never espoused as a governmental policy. Indeed, General Evren inveighed against the abuse of prisoners on a number of occasions. And the military authorities themselves investigated several hundred violations of human rights, brought a number of those accused to trial, and convicted some of having tortured prisoners.

Although the return to civilian politics in 1983 eased some of the harsher restrictions on human rights, the differences in practice from the Second Republic were stark. In the Third Republic, the press was on a shorter leash, including a general prohibition against criticizing the actions of the generals during the period of military rule. Marxist ideology could not be espoused, nor could religion be freely exploited for political purposes. In addition to these reductions in the scope of political debate, legal sanctions initiated during the period of military rule continued to be pursued against the leaders of the Confederation of Revolutionary Workers' Unions and the notables involved in the Peace Association, although some of the defendants were finally allowed the privilege (an unusual one in Turkey) of being released during the trials. Yet even after Özal took power, the limitations on free speech were emphasized by the inauguration of new legal proceedings against the 59 of over 1,300 "intellectuals" who had signed a petition calling for expanded attention to human rights in Turkey. Nonetheless, efforts to broaden the scope of individual freedom and to extend civil rights formed an undercurrent in the political contests of the Third Republic, in addition to providing grist for the mill of European criticism of the quality of Turkish democracy.

NOTES

1. See Steven Erlanger, "Turkey Gradually Moving Away from Military Rule," *Boston Globe* (November 22, 1984), pp. A12–A13, for a detailed summary of Turkey's contemporary human rights problems.

General Kenan Evren, president of the Turkish republic. His genial but firm manner was credited with providing stability to Turkey during its most recent period of military rule.

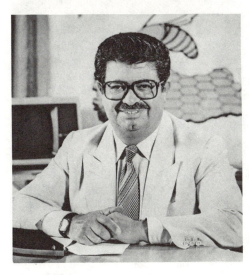

Turgut Özal, prime minister of Turkey, shown in front of the honey bee, symbol of his Motherland party.

Flushing out Kurdish dissidents in southeastern Turkey. A local villager is directing Turkish troops to an underground hideout used by Kurdish rebels.

Captured Turkish terrorists and their weapons. Generally youthful, terrorists in the 1970s included a significant percentage of women. In addition to violent acts, such groups distributed appeals to the downtrodden to rise against the regime.

6

The Role of the Military

The armed forces have occupied a special position in Turkey. Their political weight enters into party and government calculations on a range of matters far beyond military interests. The political influence they wield derives in part from their monopoly of legal force and their status as the de facto last recourse in domestic conflict, and in part from the peculiar history of the military establishment in the Turkish reform movement and their centrality in the creation of the republic.

Ottoman antecedents imbued the officer corps with remarkable status as the leading element of the state, responsible for its destiny. But the military also had a powerful tradition of subordination to civilian control that prevented any concept legitimizing military rule from taking root. By the time of the late Ottoman Empire, the divorce of the army from the political arena was called into question by the dramatic Young Turk revolution, which was led by officers. Yet the failure of military leaders to assume the top spots in the government in the early years of the Young Turk era helped ensure that civilian elements would play a major part even after the triumvirate, two of whose members were officers, took power. Moreover, the third triumvir, Talat Pasha, was a civil servant who functioned as a balance wheel between the two military rivals. Thus even the Young Turk experience did not lay the ground to establish the legitimacy of military as opposed to civilian rule.

Nonetheless, eight times in the past sixty-five years, or on the average once every eight years, Turkey has seen within the Republican era a public intrusion of the armed forces

153

into the political arena. Where the military establishment has been united in support of these interventions, they have been successful and widely accepted or even acclaimed by the Turkish populace as necessary to save the nation. Where they have been minority efforts by disgruntled elements within the armed forces, these attempts have failed and their perpetrators have been punished.

Military interventions of this frequency raise major questions about the attachment of the armed forces to their historic principles and about how they now interpret the sanctity of civilian rule. The fact that officers have taken over the government from elected politicians twice in two and a half decades and brought down a third prime minister by means of an ultimatum within the same period underlines the urgency of the answers. Indeed, it is important to consider whether this series of events can be interpreted merely as growing pains in the implantation of the democratic process or whether these interruptions imply deeper flaws that will continue to frustrate normal democratic procedure from operating in Turkey. Although no categoric conclusions are possible, a closer look at what led the Turks to these alternations of civil and military rule may give clues to the answers and allow a firmer judgment on the degree of progress that Turkey has made in its quest for democracy.

Atatürk and his chief lieutenants were all career officers when they launched the Struggle for Independence. The armed forces operated the major secular educational institutions at the university level in the closing decades of the Ottoman Empire. Indeed, the officers were the main transmission belt for Western ideas flowing into Ottoman domains during this period. As a result, the military leaders were among the most committed reformers in Turkey and formed a leading wing of the intellectual elite. The officer corps did not represent a conservative point of view in the Turkish context. Accordingly, Atatürk's reformist approach was archtypical of the outlook of the military establishment, which provided fertile ground for recruiting the backbone of the nationalist movement.

The difficult days of the Struggle for Independence and of the founding of the republic were not times in which to observe the niceties of separating military and civilian careers. In accordance with the needs of the moment, senior commanders served in parliament, on diplomatic missions abroad, and as government administrators without resigning their commissions. Atatürk depended on the loyalty of the military command structure as an essential prop for his leadership of the national movement; after he was forced to resign from his post as commander of the forces in Anatolia, it was his former subordinates who countersigned all his orders and authenticated his use of the military command network to direct the national resistance movement until the convocation of parliament in Ankara a year later. Only when Atatürk was safely elected president of the assembly could he dispense with this formality. But as the war against the invading Greek forces reached a climax, Atatürk also waged a campaign to gain parliamentary approval to add the position of supreme commander to his civilian title. Although he succeeded in both battles, his parliamentary triumph proved the least lasting as his nationalist comrades accorded him this military command only until victory in the war had been achieved. Thereafter, his dominance could be formally expressed merely through civilian channels.

In the immediate aftermath of the victory on the battlefield, political rivalries were expressed in a tug-of-war over the allegiance of the army. Atatürk felt it necessary to make sure the armed forces were behind him before taking the momentous step of abolishing the Ottoman royal house. Yet when he launched his program of modernizing Turkey through disestablishing Islam and through instituting Western laws and customs, he faced increasing dissent from some of his most senior wartime military collaborators. By 1924, a number of senior generals defected from Atatürk's Peoples party to join forces with the mounting civilian opposition.

This threat of a combined military and civilian opposition imparted urgency to the matter of separating the armed forces from active involvement in politics. Thus Atatürk ordered the commanders to choose between political and military careers. When they opted for politics, the most pressing danger was past. But even when oppositionist officers were arrested in

connection with the discovery of a plot against his life in
İzmir in 1926, Atatürk moved carefully: whereas the chief
civilians alleged to be involved were hanged (the evidence
in regard to the more prominent figures was never thoroughly
convincing), their senior officer allies were released with a
mere slap on the wrist. It was not until 1927—when the
dissident generals, having lost their assembly seats in the
elections, requested to return to active army commands to
which their rank entitled them—that Atatürk finally disen-
tangled the military and civilian services. He refused the
dissidents' request, but, at the same time, to keep a semblance
of balance, he and his closest associates announced their own
retirement from active-duty status. Henceforth, politicians
could not claim the right to return to active military duty.

Yet Atatürk, Prime Minister İsmet İnönü, and Assembly
President Kâzım Özalp continued to maintain their close
personal ties with the armed forces. As chief of staff, Marshal
Fevzi Çakmak ran the military establishment on their behalf.
He enjoyed a position of special importance, taking precedence
over cabinet ministers. In return, he took good care to keep
the armed forces out of day-to-day politics: in the 1930s, it
was apparently even forbidden for the cadets to read daily
newspapers in order to make sure that in their formative
years they were not stirred up by political events. That was
a futile gesture, of course, and it subsequently became clear
that even communists on the left wing and Pan-Turanists on
the right had succeeded in assembling a tiny core of recruits
in these forbidden precincts. The regime's efforts to inculcate
the values of the Atatürk revolution, however, elicited far
deeper response than did the competing attempts of those
of left and right extremist persuasions; compulsory courses
in the Turkish revolution profoundly influenced the thinking
of successive generations of officers. These officers were thus
well prepared psychologically to carry out the role Atatürk
continually held up for them as the ultimate guardians of
the republic against enemies of the reform effort as well as
against foreign foes.

On Atatürk's death, the soldiers had an immediate opportunity to show their colors. It was Marshal Çakmak's firm

stand in favor of İsmet İnönü that frustrated bids for power from then Prime Minister Celâl Bayar and from Minister of the Interior Şükrü Kaya. Once Çakmak had made clear that İnönü should be called back from the forced retirement in which he had spent the last year of Atatürk's life, the die was cast. Although İnönü's prestige made his succession likely in any event, the smoothness and near unanimity it enjoyed were almost certainly a result of his strong support from within the military establishment.

As part of İnönü's move toward a meaningful democracy, the special position of the officer corps was changed significantly. In 1944, the armed forces were removed from the purview of the president and brought directly under the control of the prime minister; five years later, the general staff was finally placed under the Ministry of National Defense in an effort to enhance civilian control.

These developments brought the military establishment into the normal give and take of political life: the grand isolation of the armed forces from politics that had obtained during Atatürk's lifetime was over. Çakmak himself was forced out of his position as chief of staff because of age, although he had expected to be exempted from the normal retirement requirement. In reaction, he lent his prestige to the political opposition then forming to challenge İnönü's primacy in the post–World War II era. Within the armed forces, junior officers established connections with the burgeoning Democrat party and began forming small clandestine plotting groups to protect this party if elections should not be held fairly. These groups were dedicated to a limited cause and did not put down deep roots; thus they faded away following the 1950 elections in which the opposition scored a major triumph.

On the other hand, the top-ranking officers in the late 1940s remained fiercely loyal to İnönü's government. There are credible reports that the senior commanders sounded him out on the course to be followed toward the Democrat party after that organization won the 1950 elections. In keeping with his mission to bring democracy to Turkey, İnönü was categoric in opposing any extralegal acts to prevent the new administration from taking office.

The Democrats wasted little time in changing the chief of the general staff and in rewarding their middle-level supporters in the armed forces. They followed up with legislation that prepared the ground for a gradual but broad purge of the officer corps to weed out unreliables. But having pulled the teeth of the military establishment, the Democrat party administration turned to other politically more salient sectors and virtually ignored developments within the armed forces thereafter.

THE 1960 MILITARY MOVE

Plotting among middle-grade officers resumed in the mid-1950s, but this time against the Democrat party regime. It was triggered by the mounting authoritarianism of the Menderes government, which alienated much of the reformist elite, including a sizable proportion of the officer corps. The ground was prepared in the armed forces by the dramatic decline in status and prestige of military service as the Democrats courted the peasant masses rather than paying attention to the officers who were not even eligible to vote. The Democrat leaders made no secret of the fact that the military establishment pulled no weight in the decisionmaking process. To emphasize the unimportance of the officers, the Democrat party administration allowed their pay to lag far behind the rapidly rising inflation, to the point where those in the lower ranks could no longer hope to lead a middle-class existence. The contrast between this shabby treatment at the hands of a party that lacked traditional ties to the military establishment and the reinvigoration of that establishment by exposure to the political and economic norms of NATO countries where they were sent for training intensified discontent among the officers. It provided them a new perspective in which to see the failings of the government and to appreciate the gap between democratic practice in the West and in Turkey.

Yet for all the economic hardships and slights to their honor, the officers might not have tried to carry their plotting to fruition if the Democrats had not moved in ways that appeared to threaten directly the continuation of the parliamentary system. Not only had the Democrat party leaders by 1960 come to create doubt that elections would be held, but they turned to the armed forces to restrict the activities of the Republican Peoples party. Indeed, the Democrats even seemed to be moving to outlaw the party of Atatürk. At the same time, İsmet İnönü and his Republican Peoples party colleagues made it more difficult for the officers to pursue a neutral course by attempting to maneuver the military establishment into refusing to obey partisan commands. Of course, the line of disobedience was hard to draw. İnönü's famous statement—that if the Democrats persisted in their course toward reimposing a one-party system, even he could not save them—seemed an open invitation to the armed forces to step in. It was therefore not surprising that under these conflicting pressures to choose sides, a group of colonels and younger officers took the bit in their mouths and led a revolt that brought along virtually the entire military apparatus except for the topmost ranking officers.

The military junta, having had to plan its move in utmost secrecy, had not been able to resolve the sharp divisions among its members on their future course before they came to office. Some middle-grade officers wanted a thorough remaking of society under a lengthy period of military rule. Others were merely eager for power and seemed to have given little thought about what to do once they had achieved their initial goal. But the most influential faction of the junta saw the task as simply one of "putting the train back on the tracks" with solely legal and constitutional changes. The new crop of military leaders, who came to the top of the service after most of the more senior generals were retired, concluded in short order that a prolonged period of rule by the officers would politicize the armed forces. They thus supported the junta faction, which wished to return to civilian government as soon as practical. This powerful alignment soon purged the more extreme elements of the junta in order to ensure that the regime would restore the parliamentary process without delay.

The military takeover of the government in 1960 was

broadly accepted by the Turks as justified to prevent the perversion of the democratic system. The trials of the Democrat leaders did serve to discredit former Prime Minister Menderes. They were ultimately unsuccessful, however, in destroying the political prestige of former President Bayar; the execution of Menderes and two close associates as well as the incarceration of most Democrat deputies were also harder for the body politic to swallow. Yet, although almost from the first the civilian politicians worked to prevent any executions and then sought an amnesty for political prisoners, there was no serious effort to deny the legality of the Second Republic or to seek punishment for the junta.

It was thanks to the general acceptance of the legitimacy of the military move that the return to party politics could be relatively quick. Within seven months, a constituent assembly was in operation; another five months saw a new constitution ready for referendum; and within a total of seventeen months, elections for a new civilian parliament had taken place. This success in resuming civilian political life was facilitated by the presence at the head of the Republican Peoples party of İsmet İnönü, an experienced and respected leader with impeccable military credentials as an ex-general. The fact that the Republican Peoples party leadership was not blamed by the dominant military faction for the degradation of the democratic process that had provoked the military intervention enabled İnönü and his colleagues both to foster and to cooperate in the move back to civilian rule.

Yet the course back to parliamentary process, while rapid, was not smooth. The very act of seizing power and ruling had disrupted the chain of command in the armed forces, damaged discipline, and deeply politicized the officer corps. It was not until after two abortive coups by middle-grade officers had been put down with increasing severity in 1962 and 1963 that it became clear that plotting carried such serious risks and penalties as to be all but out of the question for any but the most senior generals. Indeed, Talat Aydemir's execution for leading the 1963 putsch ended for a time serious consideration of overturning the civilian government by those below the level of the senior commanders.

Key to the willingness of the junta to leave power was the adjustment of the system to legalize a more prominent role for the senior commanders than had existed in the past. Although the military rulers, like other elements of Turkish society, basically accepted the notion that legitimacy ultimately required civilian rule, they wished to make it more difficult than before for the civilians to ignore the views of the armed forces. Hence, the junta provided that its members become permanent members of the senate; unmistakable military pressure was also exerted to see that the head of the junta was elected president of the new parliament. But the most important innovation imposed by the military leaders was to create a National Security Council, where the leaders of the armed services and the chief of staff could convene with the top civilian leadership under the chairmanship of the president to consider all matters touching on the security of the state. This provided a legal forum for the armed forces to be able to convey their views to the civilian politicians. The absence of such a mechanism was held to have allowed Menderes to disregard military sensitivities in proceeding on his fatal course.

"COUP BY MEMORANDUM"

The political system of checks and balances instituted by the constitution of the Second Republic did not lead to the healthy political life for which the military establishment had hoped. Instead, proportional representation invited those who disagreed with the major parties to split off to form their own political organizations. The guarantees of political rights put into the 1961 constitution to prevent despotism gave left and right extremists scope for action and representation in parliament. The waning of the cold war led a minority of Turks to question alliance with the West. Students aped those in France who were able to shake even such a powerful leader as Charles de Gaulle; in Turkey, they took up political violence as a way to make their mark. Disorder also spread to elements within the labor movement. Some youthful leftists even sought to dramatize their cause through sensational acts such as bank robberies and kidnappings.

The rapid deterioration in law and order impelled the generals on the National Security Council to demand more effective government. Their ultimatum to this effect, in March 1971, was signed by the chief of the Turkish general staff and by the commanders of the three armed services as well as the gendarmerie; it was sent to the president of the republic and to the speakers of the upper and lower houses of parliament, asking urgently for "an understanding above party politics." Otherwise, the generals warned, the military establishment would "use its legal rights and seize power directly to accomplish its duty of protecting and supervising the Turkish republic."

The 1971 intervention was an incomplete one. Because Prime Minister Demirel stepped down immediately and parliament installed a series of administrations led by civilian technocrats, the senior officers were able to remain in the background. The generals constituted a powerful behind-the-scenes force from which the civilian government and the politicians took their cues. And the parliament wasted no time in declaring martial law in key provinces. But all these moves were voted through established parliamentary procedures, and the generals did not formally exceed the prerogatives vested in them by the constitution.

The commanders were united in seeking to work through the parliamentary system. They recognized that by so doing they would avoid the dangers of politicizing the armed forces inherent in assuming direct responsibility for day-to-day political decisions as in 1960. And they clearly judged that the problem was a relatively discrete one: the failure of the Justice party government to declare martial law and empower the security forces to handle the violent challenge from the young. Thus, although the generals regarded Demirel's political style as responsible for Turkey's crisis, they had not lost faith in the 1961 constitutional order. Unlike the evolution of events in 1960, this time the status of the military profession and the role of the armed forces were not subjected to serious question. Moreover, the National Security Council system provided a mechanism for delivering the ultimatum in a way that could be accepted by the civilians without any need for a full takeover of the government by the commanders.

An immediate problem for the senior generals, however, lay in the presence of hotheads in the lower ranks of the officer corps. Some of their juniors apparently felt that the halfway move of the commanders was not a sufficient remedy; these officers were interested in taking direct power. The superior officers apparently talked this group out of attempting to carry out its own coup, on the grounds that the chain of command would ensure that Turkey tackled its urgent concerns decisively. But in view of the potential danger presented by these malcontents, they were retired in short order by the senior generals after the March ultimatum had been delivered. That nipped in the bud the likelihood that officers below the top positions would take independent initiative to exert pressure on the civilians.

Despite the limited aims of the generals merely to restore law and order, the transition period back to normal party competition took somewhat longer than it had following the 1960 intervention. Although the few legal changes to enhance police power were speedily enacted, the above-party regimes ruled Turkey for two years before martial law was lifted in preparation for the 1973 elections. The bounds of permissible political activity were narrowed by these nonparty governments; they closed the Turkish Labor party and brought its leadership to trial. The parties of the left were unable to resume activity immediately, even after martial law was lifted; hence they could not compete in the elections in 1973. Although none of the leaders of the major parties or of their centrist splinters was taken into custody, even the Justice party and Republican Peoples party found their scope for activity limited during the martial law period. It was not until the 1973 election campaign that they were able to return to business as usual.

As in the aftermath of the 1960 takeover, the civilian politicians exerted pressure to speed the lifting of martial law. In the end, it was a combination of their pushing, on the one hand, and the constitutional requirement to hold elections at the end of the four-year term, on the other, that accomplished this goal.

A major landmark in the course back to politics-as-usual was the successful effort by Süleyman Demirel and Republican Peoples party chief Bülent Ecevit to prevent the chief of staff, General Faruk Gürler, from being elected president when that post fell vacant in March 1973. Personal animus between Demirel and Ecevit usually frustrated their cooperation. But in this case, Demirel recognized that the new president would have the right to name the prime minister after the elections later that year and wished to make sure that a neutral figure not associated with the 1971 ultimatum would be chief of state. The Republican Peoples party leadership also had an interest in breaking the precedent that a chief of staff would automatically become president of the republic when a vacancy occurred.

The civilians prevailed in their drive against General Gürler, although they had to accept a former senior officer as president instead. Military backing for the chief of staff seemed to have wavered at this time, perhaps out of inter-service rivalries and certainly out of reluctance to push to the point of threatening a full military takeover. The compromise candidate finally elected after many rounds of balloting was Admiral Fahri Korutürk, who had retired thirteen years before to become an ambassador and whose health as well as temperament suggested that he would not be an activist.

Although the outcome was not a complete victory for the civlians, insofar as no established political leader had been chosen, the result nonetheless marked a major turning point in the relations between the military and the civilians. It was widely read as a retreat of the armed forces in the face of determined civilian opposition. The politicians thus concluded that they could face down the officers without risking a military takeover. It sent the misleading message that the military establishment was a "paper tiger'" that lacked the will to carry out its demands. In sum, the specter of military intervention in politics seemed to have been laid to rest, whereas the confidence of the civilians in their supremacy was given a strong boost. Significantly, in the aftermath of this experience, the generals could no longer count on mere words to cow the politicians.

The retreat of the armed forces from a political role was confirmed in civilian eyes by the patience displayed by the commanders in the face of nearly four months of parliamentary wrangling before the Ecevit coalition could be formed after the 1973 elections. Although eyes were subsequently turned toward the generals during the six months of caretaker regimes as Demirel sought to fashion his government after Ecevit resigned toward the end of 1974, military patience was again read as a sign that the armed forces would not intervene regardless of the provocation.

That the officers had lost their ability to take political action was further suggested by the ability of the major parties to purge the senior ranks. Demirel dismissed the ground forces commander, General Namık Ersun, on the eve of the 1977 elections, allegedly for being partisan toward the Republican Peoples party—a move that the courts ruled invalid the following year. Then, after the elections, the Justice party took advantage of the normal August transfers and retirements to shift all of the service commanders, a move again arousing strong criticism from Ecevit's party for injecting politics into the military. After Ecevit came to power in January 1978, the general staff felt constrained to issue a statement denying that the commanders were "supporters or sympathizers of certain political parties." That did not save the incumbents from being removed by the new ruling party. Ecevit broke precedent by personally chairing the work of the Supreme Military Council in February 1978 rather than merely opening its sessions as his predecessors had done. He then let the term of the chief of staff expire in March to bring General Kenan Evren to that post. Evren was appreciated by politicians for his coolheadedness and his ability to avoid unnecessary friction, thus opening the way for a new ground force commander; Ecevit then took further advantage of the regular transfer cycle in August to bring in new air force and gendarmerie commanders.

THE 1980 MILITARY TAKEOVER

Notwithstanding this impressive indication that the civilians had a grip on the military assignment process, the
regime was becoming ever more dependent on the armed
forces. After the outbreak of communal violence in Kahramanmaraş in December 1978, the civilians recognized that
they could not rely on civil authorities to keep order but
must turn instead to martial law. It was imposed first in
thirteen provinces, including Ankara and İstanbul as well as
a belt running from Adana on the Mediterranean to Kars on
the Soviet border. In part, these were provinces in which the
Alevi population was significant and, in part, provinces in
which the proportion of Kurds was substantial. The mounting
religious fervor and disorder in neighboring Iran as the
Khomeini movement overthrew the shah and established a
Shiite government in February 1979 led the Ankara authorities
to fear a spillover into Turkey. As a result, in April 1979
martial law was extended to six additional eastern provinces
mainly populated by Kurds. And when large-scale terrorist
operations were uncovered in İzmir, this remaining major
urban center was brought under martial law in February
1980. Although the martial law commanders used their powers
to suspend some of the most radical publications in areas
under their jurisdiction, the restrictions under which the
commanders operated made it impossible to stop the flood
of antiregime propaganda or to prevent violence from growing.
    This ineffective military effort to promote law and order
took place against the backdrop of bickering among the
politicians, who continued to dispute over the duration and
scope of martial law and other issues important to the armed
forces. A major battleground of political controversy was
again the contest to elect a new president when Admiral
Korutürk's term ended in March 1980. Although the officer
corps did not advance the candidacy of a sitting general, the
civilians proved hopelessly divided. The Justice party backed
conservative wing leader Sadettin Bilgiç as their choice against
the candidate of the Republican Peoples party, former Air
Force Commander Muhsin Batur, who, after nearly reaching

the total vote needed for election in a two-month long effort, withdrew from the contest. In the continuing competition, Ecevit's party named retired Admiral Kemal Kayacan, who had served as naval forces commander. But despite the Republican Peoples party's effort to trade on the prestige of former military officers against the civilian candidates put forward by the Justice party, no result could be obtained in well over one hundred rounds of balloting in the six months before the 1980 military takeover. That inability to complete the election of a president blocked other parliamentary activity, save for extending martial law every two months and voting on a rash of censure motions against the government or individual cabinet members. Not even the public urging by the chief of staff for the parties to elect a president without delay was effective in breaking this deadlock.

In addition to the mounting violence and deepening political paralysis, the injection of religion into politics by the National Salvation party powerfully disturbed the generals, who were thoroughly indoctrinated in Atatürk's secularist reform principles. The National Salvationists used their leverage to induce the normally secular Republican Peoples party early in September 1980 to join in a motion of censure that unseated Foreign Minister Erkmen of the Justice party for failing to support Islamic causes more assiduously. The generals were further shocked by the disrespect shown to the Turkish state by National Salvation party members in Konya on September 6, 1980, when party supporters conspicuously wearing green, the color of Islam, were seen on national television sitting during the playing of the Turkish national anthem. That this had been a calculated slight was all the more apparent to the commanders given that it came on the heels of the failure of the party's leader Necmettin Erbakan— the only one among the major politicians—to congratulate the armed forces on Victory Day, August 30. This lapse was compounded by Erbakan's elliptical explanation that "we are neither against nor on the side of" Victory Day, "but right inside it," words that Chief of Staff Evren immediately denounced.[1]

It was in this context, with the parties seeming almost

to dare the military to move in, that the ranking generals finally acted on September 12, 1980. They had given a stream of warnings and exhortations to the civilian politicians to pull together in the national interest, but to no avail. In mid-1979, President Korutürk had publicly called the parties to resolve their differences in view of the critical need for stronger government. Starting with his traditional New Year's message in 1980, Chief of Staff Evren appealed to the leaders to end partisan bickering and to fall in behind the government. In February, the martial law commander for the Adana region warned that "an undeclared civil war" was going on in Turkey.[2] General Evren urged the parliamentarians to unite to elect a president in May, after their deadlock was clearly apparent; two months later he prodded them to meet the urgent requirement for specific legislation to strengthen the hand of the martial law commanders to deal with violence. And finally, on August 30, he complained of the unfairness of civilian criticism attacking the armed forces for failing to restore law and order when the politicians were unwilling to close ranks to give the commanders the necessary authority.

Although it is not yet known exactly when planning for the military takeover began, this course of events suggests that the generals in acting considered themselves the last line of defense for a crumbling regime and had delayed taking action in the hopes that the civilians would find a way to impose more effective rule. It was only when the senior commanders concluded that the political structure could not meet its urgent challenges, but was instead disintegrating, that they stepped in. They saw Turkey involved in a veritable civil war, with casualties that General Evren later pointed out were almost equal to those in the major Sakarya battle of the Struggle for Independence. The senior generals felt that time was running out for legislation to complement the economic stabilization program. They feared that government paralysis, as a result of the conflict of powers of constitutional institutions, would only worsen. Moreover, the prospect of early elections, avidly sought by the Justice party, which saw its fortunes on the upswing, had been shattered early in September by the National Salvation party's retraction of its earlier agreement to join Ecevit in voting this last recourse to break the parliamentary stalemate. Beyond all this, the generals were also clearly frustrated at the politicians' effort to blame the armed forces for the continuing rise in terrorism.

The new military regime under General Evren as chief of state took care to insulate the armed forces from the corrosive effects of involvement in day-to-day rule. The commanders set up a government of technocrats, mainly drawn from civilian experts but headed by recently retired Admiral Bülend Ulusu. The National Security Council became the organ for policy decisions and the issuance of laws. The cabinet was thus primarily a body to administer the country under the guidelines of the council.

Military control through the chain of command operated smoothly. This time there was no need to purge the lower ranks of the officer corps. But General Evren at the start did caution his juniors to remain out of politics and to guard against the politicization of the military establishment. The care taken to restrict political decisionmaking to the handful of top-ranking generals demonstrated that the commanders did not want to risk a repetition of the indiscipline generated by the 1960 intervention.

General Evren's initial declaration showed that the National Security Council members diagnosed Turkey's ills as stemming from constitutional inadequacies as well as from partisan practice, but also that the generals still had faith that the democratic system could work in Turkey. Like their predecessors in 1960, they believed that a return to Atatürkist principles would permit the sound operation of democracy in Turkey. In the eyes of the generals, pragmatic, modernization-oriented, secular nationalism was the approach appropriate to prevent politicians from again perverting the process. In addition to legal and constitutional changes intended to ensure the application of Atatürkism, they saw it necessary to remove those guilty of excessive partisanship and to give Turkey a breathing spell free of violence in which to recover its equilibrium. To this end, Evren announced a six-point program to preserve national unity, restore security, reinvigorate state authority, ensure social peace, apply social justice, and reinstate civilian rule within a "reasonable" time.[3] In short, Turkey was to be saved through institutional reform.

Yet, judging that Turkey's ills were more serious this time, the generals were prepared for a longer transition period than was the case in the past. It took one year before a constituent assembly could be brought into being. Another year was required before the constitution could be elaborated and approved by referendum. A third year passed, while new parties were organized, before elections could pave the way for a civilian government to be installed by the new parliament.

UNDER THE THIRD REPUBLIC

The vision of the generals was to erect a structure that would provide for effective government at all times and prevent the parliamentary paralysis that had marked the waning years of the Second Republic. To do so, they not only adjusted the method of election of the president, which had been the single most intractable problem of the past, but they also wrote into the responsibilities of the president various unspecified powers to promote the smooth functioning of the regime. There is little doubt that they envisaged a military figure in this post, although in order to avoid compromising the democratic character of the regime they did not specify a military officer except for the first term under the new constitution. Moreover, they did not propose any language in the constitution suggesting that the armed forces would be considered the final recourse if all other organs failed, although they undoubtedly accepted that as the proper role of the military.

Experience of the past had led the commanders to conclude that a new party and new leaders were needed in addition to new rules for political behavior. Thus, while banning the old political organizations and ruling the former political leaders out of politics for ten years, the generals sought to ensure the dominance of elements that were committed to the aims of the military regime. To this end, they encouraged former General Turgut Sunalp to form his Nationalist Democracy party of retired officers and other distinguished notables who were well disposed toward the generals. Prime Minister Ulusu, after toying with the idea of organizing his own party, ran on the Nationalist Democracy party ticket as an independent, thereby further identifying this organization with the military establishment. And General Evren confirmed this identification by appealing, though largely in vain, for voters to favor this party in the 1983 elections.

Concern to establish the legitimacy of the 1980 move was integral to the transition back to civilian politics. Not only did the generals put specific language in the preamble of the constitution acknowledging the legitimacy of the "operation carried out on September 12, 1980, by the Turkish armed forces," but in provisional article 15 it was specified that no legal questioning of the acts of the military rulers would be permitted. This position was buttressed in the legal code by provisions against parties criticizing acts of the generals during their period in power and forbidding electoral propaganda on this issue.

Popular acceptance of the military intervention has been high. The respite from violence and fear for personal safety was welcomed by the populace at large. There was not even much question raised about the extensive powers granted the military commanders to arrest large numbers of terrorist suspects and others accused of promoting disorder. For the most part, those concerned with human rights in Turkey appeared to want the military merely to move faster in bringing charges against those being held, rather than to make less sweeping arrests.

There was also wide agreement in Turkey that the political process had broken down to the extent that the military intervention was justified. What had received perhaps somewhat less approval were the moves to abolish the parties of the old regime. But whereas there is a swelling demand to allow officials of the banned organizations to return to political life, currently active politicians have taken up the cause of the former parties. In the main, Turks appear to have accepted the argument that the level of mutual hostility generated by the old organizations was such that it was right to try new ones.

The conduct of the generals in office also elicited wide appreciation. General Evren was held to be personally popular; his avuncular approach was reassuring to those looking for a father figure in critical times, and his political style appeared convincing. Moreover, it was widely suggested that his popular standing was a major factor in securing the high approval rate in the referendum on the new constitution.

With the civilians back in office, the role of the military has returned to that of an influential pressure group. Its interests are defended by the president, although he no longer has active-duty status. The revamped National Security Council serves as a watchdog over security interests and presumably continues to be conservative in holding on to martial law responsibilities, which are still in force in a third of Turkey's sixty-seven provinces. There is little doubt that the views of the senior generals weigh heavily in decisions on how to treat those incarcerated for terrorist activities; their opinions are obviously important in shaping Özal's position on amnesty. In matters of law and order, the civilians no doubt follow the advice of the senior generals fairly closely. Other important military interests include access to adequate arms supplies, an issue on which the desires of the military leaders will have a commanding influence. Finally, control over the military assignment process is also an area in which the civilian politicians will probably have to defer to the ranking generals for some time to come.

Yet the number of issues on which the commanders can sway the course of events is limited in the new structure. They have little ability to encourage a diminution of partisanship, something they undoubtedly strongly desire. Although they would clearly like to see a consolidation of the fragmented political scene around two major parties, again there is no obvious course of action they can take to foster such a turn of events. Nor is it easy for them even to have a deciding influence on such questions as the legitimacy of the True Path party or whether the Prosperity party has strayed too far into the realm of exploiting religion—determinations that fall within the province of the fiercely independent judiciary.

It seems clear that, as in the past, the commanders have no interest in day-to-day supervision of the political process. Their experience in dealing with Turkey's political problems has, if anything, probably strengthened that aversion. And having turned back responsibility to civilians, the senior officers would be tempted to intervene directly in this realm only if there were a widespread consensus that the most weighty causes required such action. At a minimum, such justification would seem to require, first, a lengthy period of failure to deal with urgent problems on the part of the normal political process. If the past is any guide, moreover, a military move would come only after warning and open indications of military displeasure. Basically, the senior officers, at least, seem sincere in their attachment to the democratic process and are concerned that it work effectively. Indeed, they, like the rest of the Turkish population, still appear to accept the principle that multiparty politics and elected parliaments are the only legitimate system for governing Turkey over the longer run.

NOTES

1. *Milliyet* (September 1, 1980).

2. "Roundup of Turkish Events (January 1979–December 1980)," in İlnur Çevik, ed., *Turkey 1983 Almanac* (Ankara: Turkish Daily News, 1983), p. 43.

3. Radio address by General Kenan Evren (September 16, 1981).

Turkish marines storm out of an amphibious landing craft during the amphibious assault phase of NATO exercise Display Determination '83 at Saros Bay.

7

Turkey in the World

Turkey's basic foreign policy directions are hallowed by history. Some of the more important ones grew out of geopolitical reality. Others evolved from Ottoman experience and the legacy of the dismemberment of that extensive and long-lasting empire. Still others were instituted by Atatürk and represent his unique contribution to Turkey's operational code. And finally, some foreign policy choices came about in response to the current challenges to the Turkish state as the simple structure of the cold-war era proved insufficient. But the fundamental lines of Turkish foreign policy are so solidly based in Turkey's experience that they have remarkable staying power no matter what the nature of the government in Ankara might be.

Historically, the Turks were content to run the multiethnic Ottoman Empire through a Turkified administration that restricted itself to a minimum of interference in the affairs of the subject peoples. Because the Turks did not seek to impose their language, linguistic differences served as a natural basis for the growth of separatism in the nineteenth century. Inasmuch as the Ottoman Islamic rulers did not oblige conversion of Christians and Jews, but rather used the religious leaderships of these communities to administer their coreligionists, the persistence of strong non-Muslim religious identity paved the way for the eventual growth of nationalism by all the subject peoples. By attracting European attention, these religious communities guaranteed the continuing involvement of the West in Turkish affairs. Thus, in many respects, the Ottoman system carried within itself the seeds of its own

175

destruction. But the erosion of the empire in this way left scars that still fester. And modern Turkey has had to face the legacy of neighbors who harbor more or less bitter memories of experience under Turkish rule.

One of the obvious constants since Ottoman days has been a geopolitical position controlling the Straits of the Bosporus and the Dardanelles, which connect the Black Sea and the Mediterranean. Possession of these vital waterways brought Turkey into perennial conflict with the Russians beginning in the seventeenth century, when Peter the Great began his drive south. This czarist quest for an ice-free outlet from the Black Sea combined in the twentieth century with intense Soviet concern to keep hostile naval forces out of that body of water to prevent attack on the soft underbelly of the Crimea. With the signing in 1936 of the Montreux Convention, which regulated passage through the Straits to the great advantage of the Black Sea riparians, Moscow laid the basis to achieve both desires. Thus the urgency of the Straits issue could diminish once Stalin's project to gain physical control of this portion of Turkey was blocked by Turkish resoluteness with U.S. backing. And, although current Soviet use of the Straits for commercial traffic is substantial and rising, controversy with Turkey over passage through this waterway is infrequent.

The influence of geography on Turkey's destiny is nowhere more clear than in terms of the natural-resource deficit imposed on modern Turkey by the breakup of the Ottoman Empire. If the Turks had retained the oil-rich Arab lands they once controlled, they would have been a major oil producer with all of the implications of that status. Even if they could have sustained the claim to Mosul province that they pressed until 1925, when the British forced them to back down, the Turks would today have an income and independence that could have allowed them to cut a broader swath in the world. But having lost these areas, Turkey was left with a need to import oil that encouraged financial dependence on the West and contributed to periodic economic crises. More recently, the requirement to ensure oil supplies at tolerable prices has propelled the Turks toward new relationships with Middle Eastern producers.

Although the Turks have remained sincere in their renunciation of imperial desires, the memory of losing these territories with their extensive resources still influences foreign policy decisions. It is part of the explanation for why the Turks have proven so tenacious in their claims to the Aegean seabed. Even if the prospect of finding substantial oil deposits in the Aegean is remote, Turkish leaders simply cannot afford to be perceived as giving up once again those natural resources to which Turkey has a plausible claim. Thus the Turks have pressed to the limit the argument that the eastern portion of the Aegean basin is an extension of the Anatolian continental shelf and not a prolongation of the underpinnings of the Greek islands that dot the Turkish coast.

Likewise, the bitterness of the Cyprus controversy with the Greek-speaking world owes an obvious debt to the Ottoman past. The clash of Greek and Turkish nationalisms that attended the birth of the modern Greek state out of the Ottoman Empire in 1830 punctuated the nineteenth century. By the end of World War I, the collision reached a climax in the Turkish struggle between 1919 and 1923 to resist the Greek thrust into Anatolia and to establish a modern national state in the core area of the empire. Some of the potential for conflict was eliminated by the statesmanship of Atatürk and the great Greek leader Elutherios Venizelos (1864–1936) in arranging a compulsory population exchange of nearly 2 million people in the 1920s. But past bitterness provided a font of hostility when differences erupted starting in the 1950s.

The intensity of the current Greek-Turkish conflict also derives from the Turkish feeling of being hemmed in by Greek territorial waters, as a result of the surrender of almost all the islands in the Aegean by the Turks under the terms of the Lausanne Treaty in 1923. The perception that the adherence of Cyprus to Greece as desired by its Greek community would complete a screen cutting Turkey off from the open sea raised the stakes for Ankara in resisting this design since the 1950s. And this concern animates the recurring

Turkish fears that Athens might claim a twelve-mile territorial limit around its Aegean islands, thus putting all deep-water exits from the Aegean within Greek territorial seas. In that case, the Turks have said that they would fight to resist such claims.

A major aspect of Turkey's Ottoman legacy was the continuing concern to balance off its Russian neighbor to the north. As far back as Ottoman days, it was a cardinal principle of Turkish diplomacy to seek a powerful ally as "insurance" against its Slavic antagonist. The French and the British alternated as protectors of the Ottoman domain. This continuity was obscured only temporarily by the close relations between the revolutionary Soviet state and the reformist Turkish Republic of the 1920s. Problems with the USSR began to resurface even in Atatürk's day. From this point of view, the NATO alliance is merely the present-day manifestation of that traditional alignment. Even though Turkey has moved since the mid-1960s to lower the temperature of the confrontation with the Soviet Union, this modest "normalization" of relations has not vitiated the deep necessity felt in Turkey to keep a firm anchor in the West.

Nonetheless, since Turkey's experiences with the Europeans in the nineteenth and early twentieth centuries were mixed, Turkish attitudes toward the West have always had an ambivalent aspect. Memories of financial control exercised by Europeans through agents on Turkish soil after the Ottoman Empire went bankrupt in 1881 have made governments since the Young Turk days sensitive to infringements upon their sovereignty as well as to foreign economic entanglements. The first consideration has meant that Ankara regimes are unusually sensitive about avoiding even the suspicion that they would allow foreign forces to be based on Turkish territory. Thus, for example, they have been embarrassed by the very suggestion that U.S. forces could use Turkey as a staging area for operations in the Middle East. Although skittishness about bending to economic influence from abroad has lessened in the present climate of liberalism, it shackled all previous Turkish governments in their efforts to erect sufficient incentives to attract significant amounts of foreign

The signing of the Lausanne Treaty, July 1923, according to the contemporary cartoonists Derso and Kelin. Poincaré, Lord Curzon, and Mussolini bless the work of İsmet İnönü holding the pen at the table and looking at Elutherios Venizelos, the Greek delegate.

capital. Memories of past exploitation by European concerns induced the Turkish parliament to nationalize all mining ventures in Turkey in the 1960s and frustrated attempts in the same period to entice Western firms to renew intensive oil exploration. And with the resumption of party politics, the current turn away from autarky is already a subject for political sniping.

ATATÜRK'S NEW DIRECTIONS

Although continuing themes from the Ottoman past served as a foundation for subsequent Turkish foreign policy, Atatürk gave direction and shape to Turkey's orientation in quite new ways as well. His precept and example have remained major sources of inspiration in setting Turkey's course. Nonetheless, he was a pragmatist and an experimenter; he did not seek to bind Turkey to an ideology or to set foreign policy in a rigid mold. Moreover, Atatürk's legacy in foreign affairs was not specific enough to answer all of the questions and needs of his successors.

Among Atatürk's distinctive contributions was his determination to see Turkey evolve into a powerful Western-style modern state. Beyond his celebrated moves to westernize law, dress, and manners, he welcomed numerous German Jewish professors fleeing the Nazis in his program to modernize the Turkish educational system along European lines. To the Kemalists, education was the cutting edge of reform; indeed, it was through this means that Atatürk believed he would ensure Turkey's position as a Western nation.

The design of republican Turkey to become identified as European implied close ties with England and France in the interwar years. This orientation thus also paved the way for intimacy with the United States in the era following World War II. Indeed, membership in NATO was read by many in Turkey as confirmation of the Kemalist dream of becoming a Western state. Even the masses, who have always been far more attached to traditional Islamic forms, came to support the basic thrust of westernizing reform; their interest in the West has been vividly demonstrated by the eagerness of

Turkish workers to join the more than a million of their fellows who streamed to Western Europe in recent decades. Hence, although there has been debate over the proper timing and conditions for joining the Common Market, Turkey's basic Western alliance is solidly based on the wellsprings of the modern Turkish state.

Another major feature of modern Turkey's foreign policy associated with Atatürk was the renunciation of empire. Atatürk recognized far more than many of his contemporaries the futility of attempting to maintain a multinational state. As he put it: "In a state which extends from the East to the West and which unites in its embrace contrary elements with opposite characters, goals, and culture, it is natural that the internal organization should be defective and weak in its foundations. In these circumstances, its foreign policy, having no solid foundation, cannot be strenuously carried on."[1] As a result, the National Pact of 1920, enacted by the Ottoman parliament under Atatürk's pressure, restricted Turkey's claims essentially to its core area and renounced the idea of Pan-Turanism, which would have sought to unite all Turkic peoples of the world in one state—a sure recipe for conflict with neighboring states.

An arguable exception to the National Pact was Atatürk's move to annex the Hatay (the province of Alexandretta) in 1938. Questions as to whether its population was predominantly Turkish still persist. But its accretion finished Atatürk's ambitions for incorporating territory, albeit at the price of alienating Syria over the long run. Turkey today, however, takes special interest in the fate of the Turkish minority in Greek Thrace, the Turcomans in northern Iraq, and the Azeri Turks in Iran. Moreover, the Turkish community on Cyprus has come to occupy a unique position in Ankara's eyes as the touchstone of its responsibility to defend overseas Turkish interests.

Atatürk departed from all past practice to preach "peace" once the republic was established. His famous aphorism "Peace at home, peace in the world," which is restated in the preamble of the current Turkish constitution, remains the watchword of modern Turkey. It was, however, by no means a supine policy or one entirely preoccupied with domestic concerns. Indeed, long after the victorious conclusion of Turkey's struggle for national independence, Atatürk was willing to take risks that could have embroiled Turkey in war. For example, to solidify Turkey's relationship with Britain so that Ankara might succeed in consummating its long-hoped-for Anglo-Turkish alliance, he agreed at Nyon in 1937 to join an international effort led by the British to hunt down unidentified submarines discovered in the Mediterranean. And Atatürk's insistence on incorporating the Hatay brought Turkey to the brink of war with France in 1937. Both decisions were bolder than his principal associates were comfortable in advancing.

This boldness has been echoed, if for the most part more faintly, by his successors. The pro forma declaration of war on Nazi Germany in the waning hours of World War II gained Turkey a seat in the United Nations, even if Ankara ran little risk of having to engage in hostilities. The Democrat party government was quick to send troops under UN auspices to fight in Korea in 1950—a conflict far from home but also a venture from which the Turkish leaders hoped to earn membership in NATO. Of a considerably bolder sort was the Turkish landing on Cyprus in 1974 to secure the northern third of the island for the Turkish community. Although that has opened the way for continuing difficulties, the Turks have persisted in this enterprise despite adverse votes in the United Nations and pressure from their closest allies.

The determination to have full independence, another major legacy from Atatürk in foreign affairs, has proven ambiguous and, hence, hard to apply in practice. Atatürk himself spoke against entangling alliances, such as those in the past that had embroiled Turkey in war. Yet, to reinforce his country's defenses, he concluded two regional pacts—one in the Balkans and one with his eastern neighbors—that foreshadowed the Baghdad Pact and the short-lived Balkan Pact that his successors had formed at the height of the cold war. Although arrangements in the Balkans were stymied by problems with Greece, close relations with Iraq and Iran, with which Turkey shares a large Kurdish minority, have been a continuous feature of the Turkish diplomatic landscape. Rapidly burying the disappointment of losing Mosul, all Turkish republican regimes have pursued cooperation with Baghdad. Even the 1958 Iraqi revolution, which overthrew a monarchy with special ties to Turkey, did not disturb relations for long: Turkey soon became the only NATO power with close ties to Abdul Kerim Qasim. And in part to satisfy their interest in coordinating policies toward the Kurds, the Turks remained on strikingly good terms with each of the procession of Iraqi regimes that followed. Ankara worked diligently to do the same with the shah's governments. Once the shah was overthrown, the Turks wasted no time in attempting to build common bonds with his Islamic successors.

Even in the realm of economic independence, about which the Turks have been most sensitive, Atatürk's performance was open to conflicting interpretation. He backed the Chester Convention in the mid-1920s, an arrangement that would have given an American group of investors extensive economic rights if they had been able to raise the requisite capital to extend Turkey's railroad network. After this scheme fell through, he applauded Turkey's ability to finance its own development, rather than follow the disastrous Ottoman model of large-scale foreign borrowings. Nonetheless, in the 1930s, he accepted Soviet loans to back Turkey's First Five-Year Plan and sought economic assistance from the United Kingdom as well.

There is no doubt that Atatürk's goals in international economic relations were diversity and balance. Yet, during his era, Turkey became disproportionately entangled with Nazi Germany. By the mid-1930s, Hitler's regime had become Turkey's main trading partner in both imports and exports. The dependence of Turkey on spare parts from Germany had reached such a level that the Kemalist regime had to weigh carefully the competing pressures for and against breaking economic ties with Berlin during World War II. Indeed, so enmeshed were the Turks with Germany that the final decision to declare war on Hitler's regime was a wrenching one, even though it came only after the war was effectively over.

ALLIANCE FOR THE COLD WAR

To Ankara, there was little alternative to grasping the West as tightly as possible after the war's end. Defense against Russia was a deeply ingrained response in Turkey, despite the era of revolutionary cooperation between the new Turkey and the Soviet state in the 1920s and 1930s. The Kemalist government had made it a basic rule not to be caught in a position that would give Moscow either the opportunity or the provocation to confront Turkey. Turkish neutralism during World War II spared Turkey the burdens of active military operations or military destruction. But it was not a tactic that promised to prevent Turkey from being forced into the embrace of the Kremlin after the war; for with the defeat of the Nazis, Turkey was left faced with a resurgent Soviet regime, bent on creating buffer states around its periphery.

Although the issue of whether or not the Soviets would attack Turkey militarily had already been settled by 1947 as a result of the Turks' stout resistance to Moscow's demand for bases in the Straits and Stalin's concern lest he provoke U.S. retaliation, Ankara remained highly alive to the danger from the north. Thus the Turks were exceedingly enthusiastic about the prospect of military assistance from the United States in the Truman Doctrine. They also were particularly interested in the possibilities of receiving aid under the Marshall Plan to restore their economy, which had been seriously hurt by the cutoff of imports during the war. Once NATO came into being, first a Republican Peoples party and then a Democrat party government worked earnestly and creatively to gain admission. In those days of cold-war intensity, foreign policy was bipartisan in Turkey; the U.S. connection was welcomed by virtually everyone, except for a handful on the left.

The Turks thus entered the Atlantic Alliance without reservations or afterthoughts. The Democrat party regime was willing to take whatever diplomatic moves (such as setting up the Baghdad Pact) it felt would be pleasing to Washington. Inasmuch as the Americans disposed of ample resources to meet the Turks' urgent needs, military cooperation between

the United States and Turkey was by and large highly successful. Ankara's creaky military apparatus was revitalized
and upgraded. U.S. strategic interests were well served by a
number of bilateral operations conducted with the Turks
under the NATO umbrella. The U-2 program of reconnaissance
over the Soviet Union flown from Turkish bases was only
the most important of these successful joint endeavors. Hence
the end of the 1950s saw Turkey with military forces modeled
on U.S. patterns and thoroughly integrated into the NATO
alliance. If there was a fly in the ointment, it was the
controversial use of İncirlik airbase near Adana for the staging
of marines to be landed in Lebanon in 1958. Failure to consult
adequately before this operation or to manage public relations
during it left scars that would eventually contribute to a
narrowing of American freedom of action in Turkey.

In the economic field, however, problems in the alliance
were already more apparent. Washington sought to structure
its assistance program at least partly on the basis of economic
criteria. The United States therefore objected to the use of
aid by the Turks for partisan political purposes. Prime Minister
Menderes insisted that the U.S. program be one of general
support to his administration; he wished no questioning of
the suitability of his policies. Yet, by 1958, financial stringencies
brought him to agree on a far-reaching stabilization program
that curbed some of his economic license in return for relief
from his most acute financial pressures. His compliance with
the program, however, was not complete. And by the time
he was overthrown by the military two years later, Turkey
was already back in financial hot water.

The overthrow of the Democrat party regime in 1960
did not immediately usher in changes in Turkey's foreign
relations. Indeed, the ensuing three years were ones of good
relations in the alliance. During their year and a half in
power, the military rulers were too preoccupied with remaking
the domestic political scene to be able to devote sustained
attention to devising major foreign initiatives. Moreover, coming out of Turkey's military tradition, they were reasonably
satisfied with Washington's performance, although they did
aspire to regulate U.S. personnel more rigorously than in the

past in order to prevent abuses of extraterritoriality and to ensure the application of Turkish laws. Even those younger officers on the junta who later would become the most intense critics of the United States did not express such extreme attitudes during their months as military rulers. Nor did their civilian successors display an inclination to change the basic foreign policy positions inherited from the Democrat party.

Nonetheless, the military's entry into politics did set in train trends that eventually would have important repercussions for Turkey's foreign orientation. The broadening of the bounds of permissible political activity was accompanied by an expansion of political debate. A mood of questioning of traditional institutions swept over the political elite. At first, this probing and testing focused on domestic matters. But the rise of the socialist movement in the early 1960s was accompanied by a changing spirit in Turkish foreign policy. Early evidence that old patterns of foreign alignments might also come into dispute surfaced when Turkey finally moved to set itself squarely in the camp of the Algerian nationalists in their struggle for independence from France. But such was the institutional impetus of the alliance with the West that, even after changes in the essence of the cold war made some loosening of the bonds with the United States thinkable, it took powerful motives to move beyond the era of unquestioning satisfaction with NATO ties.

CRACKS IN THE ALLIANCE

The stage for reevaluation of links with the West was set by the Cuban missile crisis toward the end of 1962. Turkey's intimate involvement in this crisis came because the Turks, almost alone among the NATO members, had accepted Jupiter missiles at the end of the 1950s. To Moscow, the idea of a trade offered a face-saving way to back down in Cuba. So the deal was struck between Moscow and Washington: the obsolescent liquid-fueled Jupiters were to be pulled out of Turkey after a decent interval in exchange for immediate withdrawal of Soviet intermediate-range missiles from Cuba. Ankara found the whole procedure unsettling. The Turks were not consulted in the deal and no one in Turkey relished the suddenness of the confrontation in which for a few days they shared the limelight with the United States as the target of Soviet threats of destruction.

Thus the Cuban missile crisis left a double impression in Turkey. First, it cast doubt on the assumption, heretofore universally held, that being part of NATO made war with the Soviet Union unlikely. Second, and more significant, it changed Turkey's strategic weight in the alliance. Without missiles that could reach Soviet territory, the Turks no longer presented the kind of danger to Moscow that would necessitate being the target for a first strike if war loomed. That meant that the Kremlin could move away from its insistence that Turkey must leave NATO in order to have anything approaching normal relations.

If the Cuban missile crisis thus provided the necessary precondition for a major change in Turkey's foreign position, it was the Cyprus crisis of 1963–1964 that imparted the impetus for Turkey to explore a shift. To be sure, Turkey's policies would certainly have gradually evolved in the direction of focusing less on the United States in any event. The pressures of Turkish domestic politics, the increasing links of the country to world economic developments with the flood of workers to Europe, and changes of leadership in the Kremlin all would have nudged the Turks on that course. But the sharpness of the turn and the wrenching quality of the experience were directly due to the Cyprus factor, a feature of Turkish foreign affairs that has caused persistent problems for the Turks.

The necessity to act in regard to Cyprus was thrust on Turkey by events on the island, which lies some forty miles off the southern Turkish coast, visible from the mainland on a clear day. Archbishop Makarios, president of the independent Cypriot state that had come into being in 1960 by agreement of Turkey, Greece, and the United Kingdom, picked November 1963 to demand an end to the special political rights accorded the minority Turkish community by the constitution. It was a moment when Ankara and Athens were in the throes of domestic political crises. Thus, when tension on the island erupted into bitter intercommunal violence in December 1963, the Turks were quite unprepared to come to the effective defense of the heavily outnumbered Turkish Cypriots. To buy time, Ankara sent planes over Cyprus to demonstrate Turkey's commitment to its community. The İnönü government also joined the British and the United Nations in helping to stem the killings. Continuing communal troubles, however, brought the Turkish Cypriots to group themselves in enclaves, spread out across the island.

In view of the pressure on the Turkish community, Ankara considered sending an expeditionary force to protect the beleaguered Turkish Cypriots, using the authority provided in the Treaty of Guarantee that had been agreed upon by all the parties when the Cypriot state was founded. Military intervention was a bold idea but one likely to have miscarried, inasmuch as the Turks had not practiced such an operation, lacked landing craft, and would have had to seize a port to allow their troops to disembark. But before this plan could be put to the test, U.S. President Lyndon Johnson in June 1964 sent Prime Minister İsmet İnönü a harsh letter warning him that NATO might not protect Turkey if Ankara proceeded with military action on Cyprus. The Turks desisted under this compulsion, but public resentment against the United States was strong and bitter throughout the country.

Dispatch of the Johnson letter marked a major turning point in Turkey's foreign policy: Ankara's automatic diplomatic cooperation with the United States was over. The idea began to spread that the alliance might be an instrument whose primary purpose was to protect U.S. interests, interests that evidently could diverge at times from those of Turkey.

Washington sought in vain to repair the damage. İnönü was invited to discuss the issue in depth. His trip to the United States scored some short-term successes, in that Washington reaffirmed the validity of the London-Zurich accords, which included the Treaty of Guarantee. And in an effort to recoup, President Johnson proposed to send former Secretary of State Dean Acheson to mediate a Cyprus solution. Acheson very nearly succeeded in this difficult task, but his tentative accord was leaked in distorted fashion by Makarios, and

Turkey launched air strikes when clashes resumed on the island. In the end, therefore, Acheson's effort collapsed, leaving an additional bad taste in Turkish mouths. In response (and for the first time), demonstrators in Turkey chanted "Yankee Go Home!"

This phase of the Cyprus controversy set in motion several persistent trends. First, it fed the emerging leftist current in Turkey, providing the Marxists the popular issue that they had previously lacked. Anti-Americanism has been the staple of the left ever since. Starting with propaganda focusing on the United States, the leftists moved to anti-NATO slogans. And in the latter 1960s, the left launched a persistent campaign to say "No to NATO!" To a degree, this agitation even affected the Republican Peoples party, which was inclined to attribute some of its failure at the polls to U.S. opposition, as it believed that the United States favored the probusiness Justice party. Hence the Republican Peoples party began to push for greater restrictions on the scope of the alliance with the United States.

Under this pressure, the Justice party government undertook to reinspect bilateral relations with the United States after a U.S. reconnaissance aircraft crashed in the Black Sea in December 1965. Thus began an acrimonious and difficult negotiation in which the Turks sought to make clear their complete control over all U.S. activities. A new agreement restricting U.S. privileges and freedom of action was hammered out, but was not finally ratified until 1969.

A second result of the Cyprus imbroglio was the ostentatious easing of tensions between Turkey and the USSR. The Soviets at first could not believe that Washington and Ankara were truly at odds; but after Khrushchev's fall, Moscow moved rapidly to extend an olive branch to Turkey. High-level visits ensued, and the Soviets offered an economic mission to carry out several large-scale industrial projects for the Turks. Ankara was pleased at the concomitant shift of the Soviet position to a more even-handed approach to the Cyprus issue. But at bottom, the move toward Moscow did not go very far, nor did it in any way compromise Turkey's basic role in and commitment to NATO.

A third trend set in motion by the Cyprus issue was the Turkish effort to broaden its foreign interests by seeking diplomatic support in the Third World and by increasing its military and economic ties with the Europeans. Ankara was not successful in getting the Asians and Africans to shift their support from the Greek side in UN votes. The Greeks had established ties to the Arab world that proved durable in crisis. Nor were the Africans, who faced similar problems common to multiethnic states, willing to support the minority against the majority community; the precedent would have been too dangerous for their own causes.

With Europe, however, Ankara was considerably more successful. European states saw Turkey as a potential market. Turkish workers were supplying surplus labor urgently needed by the principal industrial powers. And Europe was perhaps eager to emerge from the shadow of U.S. preeminence, which had persisted since World War II, and to assert a more independent course. One feature of the European response that held special significance for the future was the identification of the Republican Peoples party as part of the family of European social democratic parties. Thus the cooperation was seen as one of kindred spirits, even though Turkey's ruling party was the right-of-center Justice party.

Turkish grievances over the failure of Washington to espouse the Turkish cause in Cyprus were only slightly alleviated by the next stage of the contest on the island. When in November 1967 a shooting incident flared up, Ankara again faced the problem of how to respond. Although the Turks in the years since 1964 had urgently sought landing craft and weapons free of U.S. restrictions, they had recorded only modest success; hence, again, they were not properly prepared to project forces onto the island. Moreover, as Athens had managed in the interim to slip some 10,000 regular troops into Cyprus, a landing would not have been unopposed this time. Fortunately for the Turks, Washington proposed mediation and sent Cyrus Vance to find a solution. After hard bargaining, he convinced Ankara to stand down and the Greeks to withdraw their illegally infiltrated troops. In Turkish eyes, this solution helped to salve the wounds of the past, for the United States in this instance was not seen as having acted inconsistently with the alliance.

As the effects of this phase of the Cyprus controversy began to fade, another major issue rose to roil Turkish-American relations: opium. By the mid-1960s, the Johnson administration had concluded that some 80 percent of the heroin illegally entering the United States was derived from poppies grown in Turkey. In keeping with the idea that allies should cooperate across the board, Washington had no compunction about raising the issue—an issue clearly not previously considered within the purview of the alliance. The Americans argued that if Turkey could not keep opium from falling into illegal channels, it must stop production altogether. Under this pressure from Washington, Ankara in 1967 acceded to the 1961 Single Convention on Narcotics, but the Demirel government was not willing to go beyond reducing the number of provinces in which poppies could be grown from twenty-one in 1967 to four by 1971. The steady U.S. pressure to cease poppy production entirely, however, caused a strong backlash among Turkish parliamentarians. With an eroding majority in the assembly, Demirel was unwilling to run the political risk of cutting back further on the area. It was thus not until the above-party government of Nihat Erim, following the Coup by Memorandum in 1971, that Ankara finally agreed to shut down its poppy cultivation. That earned for the generals' ultimatum the sobriquet "the Opium Intervention" in the lexicon of critics of the United States.

The lack of public support in Turkey for the ban on poppies meant that once normal civilian political competition resumed, it was natural that poppy production would again be allowed. Hence, when Ecevit finally formed his first somewhat mismatched coalition with the National Salvation party in 1974, an attractive action to portray the government as capable of governing Turkey effectively was to confront the United States on the right to resume poppy cultivation. Yet, to stem U.S. displeasure, the Turks agreed to change their poppy-harvesting system to eliminate the peasant from the initial processing stage—that part of the process in which diversion into illicit hands was most likely to take place. This new method all but stopped the illegal drug traffic in Turkey and removed poppy cultivation from the roster of major problems in Turkish-American relations.

THE ARMS EMBARGO

Even before this resolution of the poppy problem, the resurgence of an acute Cyprus crisis in July 1974 posed the most disruptive challenge that Turkey's alliance had ever experienced. After some years of gradually improving communal relations on the island, the military rulers in Athens mounted a coup against President Makarios. Although this action was not directed against the Turkish community in the first instance, the man who seized power in Nicosia, Nicos Samson, was known as a long-time protagonist of joining Cyprus with Greece and as a dedicated foe of the Turks. In view of his clear violation of the Cypriot constitution, Ankara asserted its right to land troops on the island, claiming that it was exercising its treaty rights to restore the status quo ante. Under strong international pressure, however, the Turks halted their military action after two days. They had followed a military plan clearly drawn up for the defense of a beleaguered Turkish community and, hence, a plan that did not call for taking advantage of the opportunity to seize the Nicosia international airport as a means to speed up their military supply. As a result, when the fighting stopped, the Turkish Army had secured only a foothold in the Kyrenia region, north of Nicosia. This failure to accomplish the goal of bringing most of the Turkish enclaves under the protection of the mainland forces set the stage for renewed military operations, with their difficult and long-lasting political consequences.

The first stage of fighting was followed by peace talks held in Geneva with representatives of the new governments that had been installed in Athens and Nicosia in the wake of the disastrous outcome of the Samson regime. But when the Caramanlis civilian government in Athens asked for a delay in negotiations in August, Turkey resumed military action in an effort to extend protection to most of the Turkish population remaining outside its sector of occupation. Having used the negotiating interval to bring in ample military supply, the Turkish Army speedily secured control over slightly more than the northern third of the island.

Although Ankara insisted that its second military operation, like the first, was sanctioned by the Treaty of Guarantee with Cyprus, Turkey found itself largely isolated in the international community. The Turks were able to generate little understanding of and tolerance for the need to have a second stage of fighting. In reaction, the U.S. Congress imposed a complete embargo on all deliveries of arms to Turkey in February 1975; this ban lasted until September but was then lifted partially after the Turks in the meantime had closed all U.S. installations and abrogated the 1969 Defense Cooperation Agreement. The embargo also prevented deliveries of U.S. weapons by all NATO countries, thus impeding the ability of other allies to replace U.S. supplies. Moreover, the European powers lent their combined influence to urging Turkey to offer concessions to the Greek side with respect to Cyprus.

The 1974 Cyprus crisis only reinforced the lessons of the previous decade for Turkey. The damage to relations with the United States, however, was greater than before. On this occasion, the Americans not only used words but took actions that punished Turkey and largely deprived it of access to Western weaponry. That weakened Turkey's defenses and increased the costs of the military hardware that Ankara was able to procure.

The Turks' first inclination was to turn to Europe as they had done ten years earlier. The Europeans were well disposed and would have liked to help. But the pervasiveness of U.S. controls made it difficult to find ways to satisfy Turkish demands. And the level of assistance that Ankara needed was in any event more than the Europeans could manage in the atmosphere of economic depression brought on by the rapid rise in oil prices. The upshot was that even with the best of wills, Europe proved unable to replace the United States as a military supplier.

Disappointment with the results of the European connection led Ankara back to explore the Middle East. This time, the Turks met a somewhat more sympathetic ear in the Arab world. Libya's Qaddafi, who was himself on bad terms with the United States, saw the opportunity to erode the Western camp by establishing a special relationship with Turkey. Saudi Arabia and Iraq, for other reasons, wished to help the Turks in a modest way. Yet Arab wheels moved slowly; they provided modest amounts of funds but had no arms to supply. Thus the recourse to the Middle East provided no adequate answer to Turkish needs, even though the effort to strengthen relations did lay the basis for a more successful drive in the next decade.

In the context of the Turkish intervention in Cyprus, relations with Greece took a decided turn for the worse. Commercial flights over the Aegean were stopped as both sides hovered on the brink of hostilities. Suspicions already fanned by the course of events on Cyprus were further inflamed by an emerging dispute over the continental shelf and air rights in the Aegean Sea. The geography of this body of water, with numerous Greek islands hugging the Turkish coast, presents complex problems in apportioning the seabed. Following the discovery of oil in commercial quantities in Greek waters in 1973, the Turks issued licenses for exploration in international waters on the Turkish side of the median line in the Aegean Sea, but in areas that Athens claimed were above the continental shelf of its islands.

Neither Turkey nor Greece, however, wished to see the dispute escalate to war. After Turkish seismic exploration in these disputed areas in the summer of 1976 raised tensions to the boiling point, the foreign ministers of both sides agreed to avoid inflammatory tactics and to pursue active negotiations. Thereafter, although no final solution was reached, tempers cooled somewhat and intermittent negotiations became the order of the day. Exploration ceased, thus putting an end to incidents that could have led to armed confrontation in the Aegean.

The Carter administration sought to promote resolution of the issues troubling U.S. relations with Turkey by sending Clark Clifford on a fact-finding mission to the area in February

1977. His trip was followed by some tangible progress in the talks between the two communities in Cyprus, which had proceeded by fits and starts since late in 1974. But the campaigning for the June elections in Turkey was not a propitious time for diplomatic action by Ankara. The death of Makarios in August 1977 added a further note of uncertainty, as did the elections in Greece in November of that year.

Ecevit's government, which came to power in January 1978, sought to impart new momentum to Turkey's foreign policy. He accorded high priority to efforts on the Cyprus issue and to easing tensions with Greece. To this end, after receiving U.S. Secretary of State Cyrus Vance, he met with Greek Prime Minister Constantine Caramanlis. Then, in April 1978, following Secretary Vance's appeal to the U.S. Congress to lift the remaining restrictions on arms assistance to Turkey, the Turkish side offered more elaborate constitutional proposals and more specific areas for territorial negotiations than ever before in regard to Cyprus. By mid-1979, the leaders of the Turkish and Greek communities were again in negotiations; yet, despite prodding from the United Nations, neither side seemed prepared to make sufficient concessions to allow for a breakthrough.

Behind this inconclusive course of Cyprus negotiations lay a new and painful fact for Turkey: starting with the 1974 Cyprus crisis, the main problem in Turkish-American relations revolved around the attitude of the U.S. Congress, not around the behavior of the executive branch in Washington. Without exception, the presidents of the United States were understanding of and had some sympathy for the compulsions that had led Turkey to act in Cyprus. But the U.S. Congress was far less willing to accept the reasons put forward by the Turks as to why they had to keep their forces on the island. As a result, it proved a difficult challenge to win over sufficient senators and members of Congress to lift the embargo on arms sales completely and to restore a high level of military assistance to Turkey. Yet the efforts of various administrations to do just that assuaged Ankara's fears to a degree and contributed to its patience in bearing an otherwise uncomfortable burden.

This contest of wills between the legislative and executive branches in Washington complicated efforts to renegotiate defense cooperation arrangements between Turkey and the United States. Stung by the economic costs of the arms embargo, the Turks insisted that economic aspects be included in any agreement. Further, to limit the ability of the U.S. Congress to restrict Turkish access to arms or to impose drastic cuts in aid, Ankara wished the accord to commit Washington to multiyear aid packages. Only in that way, they argued, would it be possible to plan for the effective use of the assistance provided by the United States. Difficult as it was to accommodate these Turkish desires, the impetus to do so was strong. As soon as the Congress had finally lifted the arms limitations in September 1978, the Ecevit government responded by allowing the Americans to return to facilities that had been closed since mid-1975. The value of these monitoring installations was such that it was clearly important to conclude the agreement within the time limit specified by Ankara for a new accord to come into force. Thus, by March 1980, a new Cooperation on Defense and Economy Agreement was signed, thereby restoring the formal relationship that had been sundered by the pressures of the Cyprus conflict.

COMPLICATIONS OF MILITARY RULE

It was at this point, with Turkey's main alliance rela-tionships on the mend, that the generals took power in September 1980. That added new complexities to the conduct of Turkey's foreign relations. The most important new difficulty arose with Europe. Already by the latter 1970s, the economic downturn in the West had begun to turn Europeans to the view that the Turks were no longer part of the solution to their labor problem, but were themselves henceforth part of the difficulty. The presence of large numbers of Turkish workers in Western Europe had generated a reaction against the Turks, who with their different customs and language were seen as an indigestible lump of very alien peoples. This growing disenchantment with the Turks was given a strong fillip by European unhappiness at the generals' takeover in September

1980. The northern Europeans, in particular, professed themselves unable to understand why the generals had stepped in; they especially seemed to view the restrictions on Bülent Ecevit as an indication of deep military disdain for democracy, and they doubted that General Evren would keep to the timetable he had announced for returning to civilian rule. Important elements in West Germany echoed these sentiments, although the Bonn government took a position supportive of Turkey. As a result, the Council of Europe was so critical of Turkey's military regime that the Turkish delegation withdrew. Economic aid from Europe slowed and European criticisms became a great irritant to Turkey. Turks complained of being rejected by the Christian West; Turkish pride and face were wounded.

This goad again turned Turkey to the Muslim world to satisfy its urgent requirements. The Turks in the latter 1970s had positioned themselves to be able to score impressive successes in developing Middle East markets. Principally through their experience in building facilities in Libya, Turkish contracting firms had gained the know-how to bid competitively. Following the construction of the oil pipeline in the 1970s to transport Iraqi oil to the Mediterranean through Turkey, commercial deals between the two countries began to rise. This trade spurted following the start of the Iraq-Iran war in September 1980, making Turkey a principal supply route for the Iraqi regime. Overcoming Iranian suspicions that Ankara preferred the shah's regime, Turkey after 1980 also expanded its trade with Iran. By March 1982, the Turkish government had concluded a commercial agreement with Iran, worth over $1 billion, to exchange food and manufactured goods for oil. And in succeeding years this trade grew even larger. At the same time, commercial dealings with Libya and Saudi Arabia increased as well; in the Saudi case, the need for Muslim skilled labor to work in the environs of Mecca gave the Turks an edge over contractors of other nationalities. Hence, by 1981, Turkish trade with the Middle East had passed that with Western Europe in value.

In tandem with this sharp upsurge in economic relations, Turkey saw the need to assume a more active role in the

Islamic Conference. Turkey had taken part in Islamic summits since these gatherings began in 1969. Turkey hosted the Islamic foreign ministers in 1976. For the first time, the Turks sent a president to attend the Casablanca summit in January 1984. Turkey also shared in the conference efforts to mediate the Iraq-Iran war. On the other hand, Ankara showed open displeasure with Israeli policies, condemning the Israeli invasion of Lebanon and various Israeli legal moves to annex Jerusalem and the Golan Heights. In response, Turkey reduced its diplomatic relations with Israel to the second-secretary level.

Relations with Moscow, in their turn, cooled considerably with the advent of military rule. The Soviet Union saw in the generals' regime a willing collaborator with Washington and doubted that the Turks could resist pressures to cooperate in military preparations for action in the Gulf area. Soviet media made much of alleged persecution of "progressive politicians and trade union activists, who are being tortured and killed" in Turkey, but who had not committed any crime.[2] Yet these public attacks were not reflected in disruption of state-to-state relations with Ankara, which remained correct.

During the tricky period of diplomacy under the military regime, ties with the United States remained the heart of Turkey's foreign policy structure. Washington's sympathetic understanding of the reasons for the military takeover, and the dimming of Turkish memories of the period of restriction by Congress of arms deliveries, paved the way for greater intimacy. The United States was in the forefront of the IMF's program to provide relief to Turkey's hard-pressed economy. And perhaps because the Europeans were so unsympathetic to Turkey's plight, Turkey's discussions with the United States over such sensitive topics as economic and military aid levels were not fraught with the acrimony these matters had generated only a few years earlier.

PROSPECTS UNDER ÖZAL

The legacy of foreign difficulties left by the generals to their civilian successors at the end of 1983 was made all the more trying by a last-minute development in the Cyprus issue. On November 15, 1983, after the parliamentary elections in Turkey but before the commanders had passed power to Özal, the Turkish Cypriot Legislative Assembly announced that the Turkish Federated State of Cyprus had come into being as the totally independent Turkish Republic of Northern Cyprus. This new creation was immediately recognized by the Evren regime, alone of all nations in the world. (Bangladesh, which initially was said to have joined in recognizing the Turkish Cypriot Republic, subsequently denied that it had extended recognition.)

Even though the military rulers responsible for this recognition went out of office within weeks, Turkey could not escape being held responsible in the eyes of the world for encouraging a step that was unanimously considered one away from an agreed solution to the Cyprus controversy. To critics of Turkey in the U.S. Congress and elsewhere, the fact that Özal would not repudiate the Turkish Cypriot move associated him with responsibility for the continuing refusal of the Turkish community on the island to rescind this action. Although the Reagan administration appealed for a reversal of Turkish Cypriot independence, it also argued for separating the diplomacy of the Cyprus issue from aid decisions to strengthen Turkey's role in NATO. But election year politics in the United States made it impossible to prevent continuing fire against this position from the legislative branch. Particularly when it seemed likely that no foreign aid bill would actually be passed before Congress adjourned in the fall of 1984, members of Congress took the opportunity to demand heavy cuts in assistance to Turkey unless positive moves were made on Cyprus. To fend off critics, the Reagan administration took the initiative to propose the establishment of a fund to promote progress toward a solution on the island, and it agreed that part of the appropriation for Turkey could go into this fund.

The clear inclination of a substantial part of the U.S. Congress to punish the Turks for accepting the independence of northern Cyprus raised anew public distress in Turkey against the United States. Although the failure of these congressional critics to prevail in 1984 and the eventual extension of a total aid package of $875 million (as contrasted with $855 million in the previous year) kept Turkish unhappiness somewhat in check, the readiness of some politicians and journalists in Turkey to vent frustrations demonstrated afresh how close to the surface grievances against Washington remained. The vagaries of foreign assistance made the Turks all the more pleased with their so-called multidirectional foreign policy. It pushed them even further toward the Middle East, whose trade relationships with Turkey were vital to the liberal economic policy that Özal had made his watchword.

Renewed difficulties with the United States also impelled Ankara to redouble its efforts to smooth out tangled relations with Europe. Özal's regime lost no time in arguing the case that with a return to civilian government, Turkey should be welcomed back into the Council of Europe. But the restrictions limiting the parties and politicians eligible to run in the 1983 elections led Europeans to question the democratic nature of the Turkish system. Thus it was only after the municipal elections in March 1984 appeared to vindicate Özal's legitimacy in a more open political contest that the steam went out of the criticism from Europe, thereby permitting Turkey to edge its way back into European democratic circles. Özal's government was still taxed with human rights violations and subjected to demands for the release of all "prisoners of conscience." But by the summer of 1984, Turkey had regained much of its lost ground in Europe, even though the alliance partners clearly felt little enthusiasm about endorsing the new Turkish constitutional regime.

A growing problem for Özal in his efforts to improve Turkey's foreign position was the emergence of a new touchstone of bilateral relationships: the Armenian issue. Demonstrations and agitation by Armenians in Lebanon, France, and especially the United States commemorating the widespread loss of life they had suffered in 1915 became large-scale affairs in the 1970s. Inflammatory rhetoric calling for vengeance against the Turks was extremely troubling to Ankara. Even more disturbing were the assassinations of Turkish ambassadors and other personnel stationed in various

Middle Eastern and Western states that had begun in the same decade. Some countries, notably France, did not respond with as much cooperation or vigor as the Turks desired. Although Ankara seemed content with U.S. seriousness in pursuing perpetrators of several spectacular acts of terrorism in the United States, gradually growing congressional interest in resolutions condemning "genocide" against the Armenians by the Ottoman Turks, as well as moves to set aside part of a proposed national holocaust museum in Washington to commemorate the killing of Armenians, struck raw nerves in Turkey. The same irritant crept into Turkish ties with some Middle Eastern states, particularly Lebanon and Syria, for the Turks suspected that those governments had allowed Armenian terrorists to be trained and supported on their territory. Thus what had been only a minor concern in the early 1970s had by the mid-1980s become a significant underlay complicating a number of Turkey's foreign relationships.

In two other areas Özal was almost completely unable to make headway. First, relations with Greece, which had stabilized by 1980 when Turkey had unilaterally reopened Aegean airspace and then dropped objections to Greek return to the military wing of NATO, took a sharp turn for the worse after Andreas Papandreou won the 1981 elections. His campaign focused in part on calls for stronger resistance to Turkey, which he claimed was preparing for hostilities. As prime minister, Papandreou set back the dialogue that Ankara had managed to start with Caramanlis's New Democracy party regime and raised tensions by authorizing new oil exploration in the Aegean. Over strong Turkish objections, he pushed the Greek demand for U.S. military assistance to be allocated according to a ratio of 7 to 10 between Greece and Turkey. And after Özal took office on the heels of the unilateral declaration of independence by the Turkish Cypriots, Papandreou upped the level of rhetoric against Turkey and canceled Greek participation in NATO naval exercises in the Aegean. It was clear that he did not consider the advent of the Özal regime to represent any basic change from the policies of the generals in Turkey.

Finally, Özal was unable to take much of the chill off

relations with the Soviets. On the surface, it was business as usual: the Kremlin continued to negotiate trade arrangements, including an expansion of some of the large joint economic projects. Yet, at the same time, the Soviets complained that "the Özal cabinet does not intend to introduce any substantial changes" in Turkey's policy from those followed by the generals.[3] Moscow expressed strong concern lest Turkey permit U.S. military forces to use Turkish territory as a staging area for "adventuristic" operations against the Middle East. The Kremlin condemned Turkey's recognition of the northern Cyprus republic, which Moscow had long believed Turkey was seeking to incorporate into NATO. Indeed, soon after Özal took power, Soviet media complained that the Turkish leadership had ignored the history of close cooperation of the 1920s and was pursuing a course hostile to the Soviet Union. Moscow Radio took up the cause of the labor leaders who were being tried for offenses during the Second Republic and criticized Ankara for the arrests of some of the "intellectuals" who in May 1984 had called for extensive changes in the Turkish human rights situation. The strongest attacks on Özal's regime, however, came in the Soviet-sponsored Turkish Communist radio transmissions from Eastern Europe, which called Özal's regime a "dictatorship" and appealed for a "massive resistance movement against the Evren-Özal duo."[4]

The panoply of problems with friends and foes confirmed the difficulties for a relatively small state to maneuver in the environment of the second half of the twentieth century. It was impossible to follow the self-reliant pattern of development that Turkish etatists had recommended for half a century. Yet interdependence was a course not devoid of painful challenges. The literal, almost mechanistic, application of treaty instruments that Ankara regimes all would have preferred also ran up against the political reality that treaty partners would not conform to such expectations by the Turks. Considerations of *realpolitik* could not be excluded from the equation. And as the world became more complex and the cold war sank deeper into the past, the levers that had produced so successfully for the Turks in the immediate postwar era no longer yielded fully satisfactory results. The middle of 1985 thus found Ankara no nearer than it had been at the end of the Second Republic to determining a course that could deal adequately with these problems. Although a multidimensional foreign policy with greatly expanded trade with the Third World offered its share of benefits, Turkey's dependence on its main alliance partners remained central to its foreign policy structure. Nor was there any obviously beneficial way to change that strategic fact even had the Turks wished to do so.

NOTES

1. This passage comes from Atatürk's seven-day speech. See *A Speech Delivered by Ghazi Mustapha Kemal, President of the Turkish Republic, October 1927* (Leipzig: K. F. Koehler, 1929), p. 378.

2. Moscow Radio (April 3, 1982); see also "Evidence of an Eyewitness," Moscow Radio (April 29, 1982).

3. Vitaliy Aleksandrov, "Turkey: Though the Government Is a Civilian One . . . ," *New Times* (Moscow), no. 4 (January 1984), pp. 14–15.

4. Voice of the Turkish Communist party (March 31, 1984), clandestine radio transmission from Eastern Europe broadcasting a recorded speech by Turkish Communist Party Central Committee Secretary General Haydar Kutlu on the results of the local elections of March 25, 1984.

8

Turkey's Prospects

Turkey's future is fraught with more than the usual uncertainties. Its political system is in transition. The return to completely normal civilian politics is proceeding, and with dispatch, but important questions remain to be resolved before the transition will be regarded by both Turks and outsiders as entirely finished. The departure from Turkey's traditional economic direction has been so sharp that the past offers little guide to the future. These challenges come at a time of increasingly rapid social change, which will test the flexibility and adaptability that the Turks have customarily shown in crisis.

POLITICAL POSSIBILITIES

How long the political transition is likely to take will be determined in one sense by the temporary provisions in the constitution and legal structure. Most of these will go out of force by the end of 1988. But the ban on political leaders of the former parties returning to political life will not expire until late in 1992. As long as these limits restrict political possibilities, the transition cannot be considered to have fully run its course. Already a number of changes to the system are under debate, ranging from restoring the voting age to 18 to ending the ban on the reconstitution of previous political organizations. More alterations are likely to be raised as time goes on, and demand will grow to deal with these as normal, rather than as extraordinary, political issues.

A natural milestone in the formal transition will be the

next general elections, which are due by 1988. Even under the constitutional and legal structure presently on the books, the coming elections will permit a far broader party selection by the populace than in 1983, as the arbitrary authority of the military rulers to veto parties and candidates has lapsed. Inevitably, some of the parties now excluded from parliament will gain representation. The next elections, whenever they are held, will therefore end the anomaly of a strong out-of-parliament opposition, even though the leaders of the banned parties of the Second Republic may not compete. If Özal's economic policies score significant progress, he might be tempted to move up the election date to extend his mandate and set back the prospect that another party could win away much of the right of center. Should the economy weaken, however, the opposition might press for early elections, although Özal in that event would almost certainly resist advancing the date in order not to run the risk of a radical shift in Turkey's political complexion.

The amount of time needed to work out other issues that impart a transitional cast to the regime is hard to predict. Ending martial law and lifting states of emergency are integral to the return to normal political process. Success in gradually reducing these extraordinary measures, and ultimately in ending them, depends directly on the ability of the regime to prevent a resumption of disorder or political violence. Özal is committed to political normalization. Already most crimes in the provinces under martial law are being tried in civilian, not military, courts. And the number of provinces under these extraordinary regimes has been significantly cut back. As time passes, if the regular security forces prove able to maintain a reasonable degree of order, political presures to abolish martial law entirely will become irresistible. Although it will take years to instill enough confidence to complete this process, a logical terminal date could be the opening of the campaign for the next general election. The demand to hold these contests under the most normal conditions possible will then be very strong indeed. But even this consideration might not prevail if threats to security were visibly rising.

A second major matter is the question of amnesty for

those jailed during the period of military rule and the restoration of full political rights to pre-1980 political leaders.
It is possible, but not likely, that parliament will move to
change the constitution to speed the return of Ecevit and
Demirel to political life. At least until the end of 1989, while
President Evren still holds a virtual veto over this process,
the assembly almost certainly will lack both the interest and
the voting unanimity to accomplish this change. Only after
the second general elections of the Third Republic, when
those more strongly sympathetic to the old regime are likely
to be better represented in parliament and when the president's
veto can be overridden by a simple majority, is a concerted
effort to hasten the rehabilitation of the former leaders imag-
inable. Yet because the temporary provisions themselves are
scheduled to lapse soon thereafter, the deputies may not be
willing to risk military displeasure to advance the process
marginally. The urgency felt in the 1960s to ignore military
objections to restore rights to former President Bayar and
other Democrat politicians who otherwise faced being deprived
of them for life would not exist in the present case.

On the other hand, amnesty for those in jail is clearly
seen as a more compelling issue. Statistics on the numbers
of those jailed for participation in illegal causes show that
over 40,000 were arrested for membership in leftist, Kurdish,
or rightist organizations. Of these about half are still in jail
(some 12,000 having been convicted and 8,000 still awaiting
trial in mid-1984), and most were apparently under age 30.
How many of those still incarcerated were convicted of merely
spreading propaganda or the like and not for participating
in actual terrorism is not clear. Propaganda offenses may be
the crime of the majority of those behind bars. According to
the current constitution and legal code, amnesty for some of
these prisoners may be possible; but relief for those who
engaged in terrorist acts or who sought the breakup of the
Turkish state cannot be considered. Indeed, judging from the
continuing interest even by Motherland party deputies in
enacting some form of amnesty for those accused of lesser
crimes, limited pardons are likely to be granted eventually.
Özal himself will probably delay early action, as he recognizes

the political risk of moving too fast on this issue. Many in Turkey believe that the broad amnesty of 1974 fueled the rapid rise of political violence in following years; in particular, those in charge of security seem reluctant to risk a repetition by letting back on the street substantial numbers of persons previously involved in any way in fostering the breakdown of law and order.

The question of the role of the military also overhangs political development. Nowhere in the constitution or among the laws is it formally set forth that the presidency will be allocated to a former senior officer. But the function of the chief of state to be commander in chief of the armed forces and to serve as presiding officer of the National Security Council suggests that the incumbent will have a most intimate connection with the military establishment. Accordingly, former ranking officers will always seem likely to be the strongest candidates for this post. Indeed, the wording of the constitution might even permit Evren to succeed himself for a second term, inasmuch as he came to the position through the nationwide referendum on the constitution rather than by the votes of parliament (that being the method set by the constitution for election to non-reelectable terms).

Finally, some broadening of the political spectrum may become an issue in the transitional process. Already the Prosperity party is pushing to the limits its appeal to the religiously oriented. In addition, moves may come to restore the voting bloc that backed the Nationalist Action party, even if necessarily shorn of its "Commando" auxiliary. A recrudescence of anything resembling a protofascist organization would be unsettling to many Turks. But the vagueness of constitutional prohibitions might permit some figures to emerge who could galvanize this previously growing constituency. And under the most favorable circumstances, a party representing these interests might be able to win enough votes to exceed the barriers to elect deputies. Turkeş's legal responsibility for the Nationalist Action party's past excesses almost certainly removes him as a possibility to return to active political life, however.

Similarly, the place on the spectrum to the left of the

Social Democracy party is likely to attract contenders. İsmail
Hakkı Aydınoğlu has begun efforts to form a Democratic Left
party. He has sent out requests to some 20,000 potential
founders in an attempt to give the intended organization the
aura of mass support. Bülent Ecevit's wife, Rahşan, has also
emerged as a potential leader of this political movement, in
a bid to enlist the support of former members of the Republican
Peoples party. But as of mid-1984, no formal party of this
sort had yet materialized.

Carefully skirting the many prohibitions on Marxist or
class-oriented parties, leaders who want to vie for support
of the left wing can probably engage in some form of activity
without running afoul of the law. Whether for some years
there will be enough of a constituency to permit a frankly
left party to win parliamentary seats is doubtful, especially
as the more extreme left has always shown a great inclination
to split into bitterly competing fragments. Yet the very effort
by such groups to become active could prove politically
destabilzing, as it would arouse reaction among those who
fear the left and would encourage political activism by extremist supporters. Indeed, lowering the voting age to 18, as
some politicians desire, could stimulate this trend by bringing
in a more extreme group of voters on both the religious right
and the doctrinaire left.

Despite these questions and uncertainties, the transition
to a normally functioning democratic system is proceeding
apace. How different the essence of the new system will look
from the pre-1980 system is still hard to tell. No party is
likely soon to achieve an absolute majority of the vote, even
if the new structure does give the plurality party a good
chance to receive a majority of seats in parliament. Only if
after an election or two most of the minor parties are squeezed
out, either by legal provisions requiring them to participate
in elections or by discouragement when they fail repeatedly
to cross the barriers to elect deputies, would the chances of
a major party to represent a true majority of the electorate
improve. The persisting fragmentation of the political scene,
however, makes it perhaps more likely that a third or fourth
party will secure parliamentary representation and thus remain

in contention, possibly even necessitating a return to coalition politics. Thus parliamentary uncertainties are sure to continue despite the effort at electoral engineering of the present system.

In any event, the smooth operation of politics in Turkey will require a maturity of political leadership and an establishment of norms of constructive interaction between the parties that were not in evidence before 1980. There is a general awareness of the need for cooperation on national issues, and some of the major political leaders have openly acknowledged the need to dampen political rivalries. Nonetheless, the temptation to return to partisan wrangling runs deep. Already charges and countercharges against national leaders have agitated the political waters over such minor matters as the municipal elections in the small municipality of Ağrı in extreme eastern Turkey, elections that were rerun in August 1984 to break an original tie vote. The rhetoric of political debate has not changed significantly from that of the last experiment in democratic rule. And the atmosphere of a continual election campaign does not add to the likelihood of political cooperation except by the outs in opposing the party in power.

Whether the new system will run into major difficulties probably depends more on whether there is a renewed upsurge of political violence than it does on any other factor. The political leadership, however, is so sensitized to the consequences of failing to respond forcefully that it would probably cooperate willingly across party lines to apply tough security measures—cooperation that might well not come on any other issue. Even in these instances, as witness the security sweep in eastern Turkey in the fall of 1984, the opposition would not be reluctant to criticize the government for letting law and order deteriorate to the extent that extraordinary measures were necessary. In this spirit of party competition, it will be difficult to achieve sufficient political consensus on basic approaches to tackle the root causes of violence. Resolute police action can deter random violence, prevent communal conflict, and forestall ethnic separatism. Inasmuch as violence feeds on itself, prevention is a significant part of the cure. Yet, in the long run, increased economic opportunities and promotion of broadened educational possibilities may also be important in removing the impetus for violence. Given Turkey's present state of political rivalries, however, it will not be easy to reach accord across party lines on exactly how to proceed in these matters. The Higher Education Council law, for example, has proven one of the most contentious of the past few years, and even this law seems directed perhaps more at prevention than at cure.

Deliberate political terrorism by small committed bands of conspirators is more difficult both to deter and to remedy than is more generalized political violence. In the Turkish case, this is especially true given that such conspirators may receive both sanctuary and support from elements in the Turkish community in Germany and elsewhere abroad. General disapproval of terrorism by the populace inside of Turkey may be helpful in restricting the numbers of those inclined to try to foment disorder by these means. But at least as long as memories of past attempts remain vivid, there are sure to be efforts at repetition. Experience either in Turkey or elsewhere gives little guidance on how to remove the impetus for terrorist groups once started. Thus vigilance, for a long time to come, seems certain to be required.

As long as the regime is relatively able to maintain law and order, the chances that the military establishment would become sufficiently disenchanted with the existing system to press for its change do not seem high. The officer corps in Turkey has shown itself to be moved only by the most serious challenges to the regime to enter the political realm. Having just surrendered the reins of power, the generals would be especially reluctant to confess that their system was unable to meet its tests, at least without an extremely compelling cause. Beyond maintaining law and order, the military establishment has a strong interest in protecting national unity, ensuring a sufficient share of national income to undergird a credible defense effort, and preventing the politicization of the officer corps through civilian interference. The officers have also demonstrated their concern over egregious backsliding against Atatürk's secular reforms and over extreme bickering among the politicians threatening political paralysis.

In the absence of challenges in these areas, the Turkish armed forces seem unlikely either to flex their political muscles or to use their residual power to intervene.

Another factor that will influence Turkey's course, however, is the state of its international relationships. The Cyprus issue continues to lie at the heart of Turkey's foreign difficulties: Its spillover into complicating relations with Greece affects support for Turkey in Europe. And the U.S. Congress perennially focuses on the slowness in achieving an agreed solution on Cyprus and the increasing separatism of the Greek and Turkish sectors as reasons for cutting military aid to Turkey. That not only disturbs Turkey's constellation of foreign relations but also plays on the domestic balance of forces within the Turkish political scene. A sharp turn in the diplomacy of this issue could cause a cycle of action and exaggerated reaction in Turkey's larger alliance structure, thus engaging national pride on all sides in a destructive downturn. Past experience has shown how little effect blunt pressure can have in gaining Turkey's compliance. Yet, until and unless the Cyprus issue moves significantly toward solution, important uncertainties will remain in Turkey's foreign relationships.

ECONOMIC OUTLOOK

Clearly, Turkey cannot escape the impact of world trends. If the Turkish state is linked politically to its Western allies, it is no less intimately bound to the global economic structure. Not only will Turkey remain dependent on vital imports to keep its economy operating, but it will also be extremely sensitive to changes in the foreign climate that affect export quotas, remittances, and Turkey's burgeoning contracts for work abroad. Thus changes in world energy prices, to single out the most salient example, will have strong, direct, and immediate impact on the Turkish economy as a whole. In this situation, the relative efficiency of Turkish enterprise as compared with those in the rest of the world will have much to say about the health of the Turkish economy, even if the current heavy emphasis on a free-market approach should be modified as a result of changes in the domestic political lineup.

The shift in recent years toward export orientation is likely to be permanent, no matter what the general philosophy of the governing party. All the major political groups recognize the value of foreign earnings in enhancing independence from international lending organizations and from government-to-government aid, which may fluctuate for political rather than economic reasons. Moreover, Turkey's success in gaining contracts abroad is so widely appreciated that the effort in this direction, too, is likely to continue. But under a left-of-center regime, the profits to owners might be more heavily taxed and subsidies that increase the competitive position of Turkish firms could be reduced in order to cut back the disparity in earnings between these large entrepreneurs and the rest of Turkey's citizenry. In the end, such measures might affect the rate of growth of Turkey's foreign economic activities, even though that would not be the intended aim.

Inflation remains one of Turkey's most stubborn problems and one for which the remedies are not easy to devise, even when the political will is in evidence. To a degree, the money supply seems to have escaped government control. With the current banking system, the government has found it difficult to control credit; no way has yet been devised to prevent the central system from printing money at an extremely rapid rate. In addition, the continued adjustment of the Turkish lira, while helping to make Turkish products competitive abroad, has contributed to boosting inflation at home. Wages have declined in real terms over the past decade to the point where the pressure to keep salaries indexed to inflation is hard to resist by politicians who depend on voter satisfaction for reelection. Thus inflation seems destined to pose a continuing threat to Turkey's economic well-being.

Unemployment will challenge the best efforts of any government in Turkey. Additional opportunities to export labor are drying up, whereas pressures to send overseas workers home from Europe are mounting. Meanwhile, the population increase is putting a million new entrants a year into the employment market. Underemployment in the agricultural sector is likely to rise, inasmuch as some prefer minimal work on the farm over the tribulations and costs of city life. But Turkey's somewhat antiquated industrial sector cannot absorb all the new aspirants, nor can service industries expand fast enough to accommodate the newcomers. The regime's commitment to rationalize the operation of state industrial concerns also reduces its ability to sop up excess labor. Hence Turkey's already high unemployment rate seems destined to remain a problem for the foreseeable future.

The State Economic Enterprises also pose continuing challenges to the government. Özal's repeated promises to reduce their deficits and put them on a pay-as-you-go basis demonstrate his attention to the problem. But the need for constant reassurances also suggests that the matter is far from being completely resolved. At best, progress can be made by slowly bringing employment into line with actual needs through attrition and by restricting new hiring. The matter of eliminating subsidies will also be fraught with difficulties, because the regime has clear political interest in not letting any of these enterprises go under. Plans to sell shares to the public would work only for the better managed and inherently profitable concerns; the sale of Bosporus bridge bonds was immediately oversubscribed. Yet the disposal of these money-making enterprises would not produce enough funds to reduce seriously the drain on the treasury of the others. Thus the obstacles to a radical resolution of the problems of the economic enterprises remain daunting.

How persistent the government will be in pursuing the rationalization of the State Economic Enterprises will relate to the general success of Özal's economic approach and the state of the grand economic debate in Turkey between the etatists and the proponents of free enterprise. Although events of the past five years have given the latter the best of the argument, renewed debate now concentrates on the persistence of inflation, unemployment (especially in enterprises focused on the Turkish market), and the growing disparity between the living standards of senior private-industry managers and owners on the one hand and the vast majority of Turks in the public and private sectors on the other. Given the deep historical roots of this debate and the difficult structural problems of the Turkish economy that defy early or easy solution, the controversy over the proper approach and mix between the public and private sectors will almost certainly form the staple of economic controversy as well as political debate for a long time to come. And public enterprises, in particular, will be severely buffeted by changes in approach when and if ruling parties shift in Turkey or the world economic environment fluctuates.

An emerging point of argument among the major political parties concerns the strategy for promoting regional balance in economic development. Although complaints continue to be voiced over the share of investment in eastern Turkey, fortuitously all the major contenders for power favor the construction of the Atatürk dam on the Euphrates river as a major tool in this effort. This government endeavor will provide jobs, agricultural stimulus, and abundant power for the perennially stagnant economy of southeastern Turkey. Success in securing a measure of European credit for the proposed turbines gives promise that the venture will eventually be effective, even though a significant part of the financing has not been worked out nor has agreement been reached with Syria and Iraq on water-sharing. The project will also answer some of the demands from the Kurdish population of the affected area for major development projects. But even if pursued with greater urgency, it will inevitably fail to still the rising tide of expectations in this deprived area of the country.

SOCIAL TRENDS

All the while that Turkey is facing these political and economic uncertainties, it must also cope with rising social dynamism. The flood of people into the cities has expanded the middle class, although the economic potential of the newcomers is not keeping pace with their rising social status. But even in the villages, exposure to modern ways is increasing. Traditional Turkey of a generation ago is progressively being transformed into a less parochial and more national- and international-minded society. Many rural Turks have traveled abroad, some to the West and some to make the pilgrimage in Saudi Arabia or to work in Islamic countries. Politicians are under increasing compulsion to meet the expanding needs of the rural sector. That process promises that rural-urban differences will eventually narrow, even if the cities monopolize a higher standard of living as they inevitably do in all countries. But Turkey is nonetheless slowly evolving in the direction of a somewhat more unified national culture than it possessed in the past.

In this process of social homogenization, modern Western values are competing with Islamic mores. On the one hand, there is more visible evidence of Islam in the daily life of the city than there had been in Atatürk's day or even a generation ago. Women with scarves over their hair and full-length dresses or coats even in summer (as a compromise between traditional modesty and dressing in Western style) are frequently seen in Turkey's major cities. They now occasion little comment from the elite, which no longer seems as bent on modernizing women's dress as in the past. Controversies over topless bathing and whether or not to restrict alcohol sales are current battlegrounds for the struggle to define acceptable limits of Islam on Turkish behavior. But dress is clearly going to be a losing battle for Islam in Turkey; the minister of tourism had to back down on his ban on topless bathing, and most of the city-born generation will not follow their mothers' bundled-up style. Even though the Islamic elements of Turkish social custom may appear striking when compared with Western European practice, those observers coming from the Middle East see Turkey as irrevocably Western in appearance. Thus it seems evident that the main surge of change is directed not toward the pervasive Islamization of the elite, but toward the modernization of traditional Islamic style practiced by the remainder of the populace.

In the process of bringing to Turkey the accoutrements of twentieth-century life, the country is developing a new generation of talent. Not only are more of the young exposed to school, but the knowledge they are acquiring is increasingly sophisticated. Some of the newspapers in Turkey have long been devoted to popular education. In the past few years, this exercise has gone to the point where achievement tests as well as college entrance examinations in science, mathematics, and related disciplines are regularly published. That not only testifies to the increasing rigor of the modern educational process, but it also offers the opportunity to youth at large to sharpen these skills. The snowballing of technical sophistication suggests that the young in Turkey are likely to be more ready to adapt to the requirements of modern life than was the next immediately preceding generation, even though it will remain the middle-aged and older segments of the populace who keep their grip on the levers of power.

~~Overall, then, although~~ Turkey faces manifold problems, there is ~~good~~ reason to believe that it will eventually achieve the stability its people are seeking. Generally flexible in their approach, the Turks show an ability to try new ways when the old ones are ~~blocked~~. They have the resources ~~in~~ talent ~~and matériel~~ to succeed in the challenging business of modernizing their society ~~and polity~~. The smoothness with which they have come back from political chaos and military rule is impressive. It indicates ~~a permanence to~~ Turkey's commitment to develop ~~under~~ representative government, ~~thus auguring well~~ for the future however many uncertainties remain.

Selected Bibliography

As is appropriate for an English-speaking audience, most of the readings listed in this section are written in English. They represent a fair summary of the current state of understanding of Turkish reality. Additional studies in Turkish and other foreign languages would not only consume enormous space but also far surpass the aims of the present volume, without contributing a greatly enlarged view of the subject matter.

CHAPTER 1: The Land and the People

For a discussion of Turkey's physical and cultural geography, see Richard F. Nyrop, ed., *Turkey, A Country Study* (Washington, D.C.: Government Printing Office, 1979); and John C. Dewdney, *Turkey: An Introductory Geography* (New York: Praeger Publishers, 1971). Most useful also is the *Türkiye İstatistik Yıllığı 1983 Statistical Yearbook of Turkey*, published in both Turkish and English by the Prime Ministry State Institute of Statistics. For information on Turkey's rural culture, see Paul J. Magnarella, *The Peasant Venture: Tradition, Migration, and Change Among Georgian Peasants in Turkey* (Cambridge, Mass.: Schenkman, 1979); Paul Stirling, *Turkish Village* (London: Weidenfeld & Nicolson, 1965); John F. Kolars, *Tradition, Season, and Change in a Turkish Village* (Chicago: University of Chicago Press, 1963), which deals with an area near Antalya that is undergoing rapid change; and Joseph S. Szyliowicz, *Political Change in Rural Turkey: Erdemli* (The Hague: Mouton, 1966), which addresses the challenge of modernity in Turkey's Mediterranean region, one of the fastest developing areas of the country. Peter

Benedict, Erol Tumertekin, and Fatma Mansur, eds., in *Turkey: Geographic and Social Perspectives* (Leiden: E. J. Brill, 1974), have compiled essays treating change in both rural and urban Turkey. The dynamic factor of population movement is explained by Brian W. Beeley in *Migration: The Turkish Case* (Milton Keynes, U.K.: Open University Press, 1983). The extremely significant process of integration of rural elements into urban life is inspected by Kemal H. Karpat in *The Gecekondu: Rural Migration and Urbanization* (London: Cambridge University Press, 1976). Aspects of the pervasive role of Islam in Turkish life are elucidated by Binaz Toprak in *Islam and Political Development in Turkey* (Leiden: E. J. Brill, 1981). Insights into dervish culture in Turkey are found in Talât S. Halman and Metin And, *Mevlana Celaleddin Rumi and the Whirling Dervishes* (İstanbul: Dost Yayinlari, 1983). Çigdem Kağıtçıbaşı, in *The Changing Value of Children in Turkey* (Honolulu: East-West Population Institution, 1982), analyzes fertility. The fundamental matter of women's changing roles is evaluated in Nermin Abadan-Unat, ed., *Women in Turkish Society* (Leiden: E. J. Brill, 1981). The strains of modernization are also considered in Frank A. Stone, *The Rub of Cultures in Modern Turkey* (Bloomington: Indiana University Press, 1973).

CHAPTER 2: THE TURKS THROUGH HISTORY

No entirely satisfactory general treatment of the Turks exists in any language. Stanford J. Shaw's extremely detailed *History of the Ottoman Empire and Modern Turkey*, in two volumes—*Empire of the Gazis* (London: Cambridge University Press, 1976) and *Reform, Revolution and Republic*, coauthored by Ezel Kural Shaw (London: Cambridge University Press, 1977)—contains a mine of data on the events it chronicles. Roderic H. Davison's brief *Turkey* (Englewood Cliffs, N.J.: Prentice-Hall, 1968) presents a more dynamic elucidation of the themes of the Turks in history. In *The Cambridge History of Islam* (London: Cambridge University Press, 1970), Halil İnalcik, Kemal H. Karpat, Uriel Heyd, P. M. Holt, and Osman Turan survey the fortunes of the Turks. Read together, these three works provide a good general sense of the sweep of Turkish experience until the last decade. Bernard Lewis's *The Emergence of Modern Turkey* (London: Oxford University Press, 1961), previously the standard account, ends on the eve of the 1960 military takeover and has been largely superseded in its understanding of the early years of the Ottoman Empire. It is still especially valuable for its lengthy section on the Young Turks, however.

Regarding the coming of the Turks to Anatolia, Claude Cahen's masterful work, *Pre-Ottoman Turkey: A General Survey of the Material and Spiritual Culture and History, 1071–1330* (New York: Taplinger, 1968), serves as a reliable guide. Rudi P. Linder, in *Nomads and Ottomans in Medieval Anatolia* (Bloomington: Indiana University, Research Institute for Inner Asian Studies, 1983), convincingly demonstrates the limitations of the role of the *gazis* in the creation of the Ottoman state. The early years of the empire are well described in Halil İnalcik's *The Ottoman Empire: The Classical Age, 1300–1600* (London: Weidenfeld & Nicolson, 1973). Niyazi Berkes, in *The Development of Secularism in Turkey* (Montreal: McGill University Press, 1964), develops material not generally used by others to produce a stimulating and original account of the middle and later periods of Ottoman rule. Carter V. Findley, in his *Bureaucratic Reform in the Ottoman Empire: The Sublime Porte, 1789–1922* (Princeton, N.J.: Princeton University Press, 1980), examines the evolution of the civil service during the famous Tanzimat reforms and their aftermath in terms of both personnel and institutional change. The standard work on the later Tanzimat years is Roderic H. Davison's *Reform in the Ottoman Empire, 1856–1876* (Princeton, N.J.: Princeton University Press, 1963). Intellectual trends are surveyed in Şerif Mardin's *The Genesis of Young Ottoman Thought: A Study of the Modernization of Turkish Political Ideas* (Princeton, N.J.: Princeton University Press, 1962). The politics of the overthrow of Abdül Hamid II are capably analyzed by Feroz Ahmad in *The Young Turks: The Committee of Union and Progress in Turkish Politics, 1908–1914* (London: Oxford University Press, 1969). The complex diplomacy of the Ottoman Empire during World War I is treated by Ulrich Trumpener, *Germany and the Ottoman Empire, 1914–1918* (Princeton, N.J.: Princeton University Press, 1968); by Harry N. Howard, *The Partition of Turkey: A Diplomatic History, 1913–1923* (Norman: University of Oklahoma Press, 1931); and by F. G. Weber, *Eagles on the Crescent: Germany, Austria and the Diplomacy of the Turkish Alliance, 1914–1918* (Ithaca, N.Y.: Cornell University Press, 1970). Finally, various topics in Ottoman history are explored in the conference proceedings edited by Osman Okyar and Halil İnalcik, *Social and Economic History of Turkey (1071–1920)* (Ankara: Meteksan Limited Şirketi, 1980).

The first decade of the Turkish Republic has not been as intensively studied as has Atatürk's role in the Struggle for Independence. Lord Kinross (Patrick Balfour) offers a somewhat fictionalized portrait of Turkey's great leader, including dialogue that was mostly invented, in *Atatürk: A Biography of Mustafa Kemal, Father of Modern Turkey* (New York: William Morrow, 1965). Atatürk gave his own account of the Struggle for Independence in his monumental seven-day speech in 1927; see *A Speech Delivered by Ghazi Mustapha Kemal, President of the Turkish Republic* (Leipzig: K. F. Koehler, 1929) for an official, but at times inaccurate, translation of this oration. Uriel Heyd, in his *Language Reform in Modern Turkey*, publication no. 5 (Jerusalem: Israel Oriental Society, 1954), considers one of Atatürk's most far-reaching reforms—one that, indeed, has not yet run its course. George S. Harris investigates a competing movement that has persistently provoked ideological ferment in *The Origins of Communism in Turkey* (Stanford: Hoover Institution on War, Revolution, and Peace, 1967). Walter F. Weiker covers Atatürk's tame opposition in his *Political Tutelage and Democracy in Turkey: The Free Party and Its Aftermath* (Leiden: E. J. Brill, 1973), but does not set this experiment in the context of its antecedents. Kemal H. Karpat's *Turkey's Politics: The Transition to a Multi-Party System* (Princeton, N.J.: Princeton University Press, 1959) stresses the transition to political competition in the 1940s and also provides a useful section on ideological developments. Richard D. Robinson in *The First Turkish Republic: A Case Study in National Development* (Cambridge: Harvard University Press, 1963) sketches an overview of the First Republic to lay the groundwork for arguing that the 1960 military takeover was unjustified and that "Turkey awaits its second Mustafa Kemal." The Atatürk Centennial Issue of the *Journal of the American Institute for the Study of Middle Eastern Civilization,* vol. 1, nos. 3 and 4 (Autumn–Winter 1980–1981), was entirely devoted to aspects of Atatürk's Turkey.

The Second Republic has been relatively well studied. Feroz Ahmad provides the most detailed account of the period up to 1975 in *The Turkish Experiment in Democracy, 1950–1975* (Boulder, Colo.: Westview Press, 1977). But he, like others, does not sound the themes that would prepare the reader for the paralysis of Turkey's political machinery in the face of rising terrorism. C. H. Dodd's *Politics and Government in Turkey* (Berkeley: University of California Press, 1969) covers the early years of the Second Republic. Jacob M. Landau carries the picture only a few years further in his rather static treatment of a dynamic problem in *Radical Politics in Modern Turkey* (Leiden: E. J. Brill, 1974). Aspects of political practice in the middle years of the Second Republic are analyzed by Kemal H. Karpat, ed., *Social Change and Politics in Turkey: A Structural-Historical Analysis* (Leiden: E. J. Brill, 1973). The generals' explanation of the social and political challenges that impelled them to act is presented in the publication of the General Secretariat of the National Security Council entitled *12 September 1980 in Turkey—Before and After* (Ankara: Ongun Kardeşler, 1982). The growing protofascist movement in Turkey was analyzed in Jacob M. Landau, *Pan-Turkism in Turkey: A Study of Irredentism* (Hamden, Conn.: Archon Books, 1981). Ideological developments are illustrated by material presented by Kemal H. Karpat, *Political and Social Thought in the Contemporary Middle East*, rev. ed. (New York: Praeger Publishers, 1982).

Although the Third Republic has not received significant scholarly attention as yet, the military regime that preceded it and efforts to return to parliamentary procedure are detailed in C. H. Dodd's *The Crisis of Turkish Democracy* (North Humberside, U.K.: Eothern Press, 1983). The background and structure of the constitutional machinery of the Third Republic are considered in Frank Tachau's *Turkey—The Politics of Authority, Democracy, and Development* (New York: Praeger Publishers, 1984).

CHAPTER 3: EVOLUTION OF THE ECONOMY

Long the standard work on the Turkish economy, Z. Y. Hershlag's *Turkey, The Challenge of Growth* (Leiden: E. J. Brill, 1968) is by now thoroughly out-of-date. Its coverage of the First Republic and the early years of the Second, however, is still valuable. Essential background to understand Turkey's foreign debt problem is found in John White's *Pledged to Development* (London: Overseas Development Institute, 1967). Also extremely useful, given its insights into the Turkish economic background, is the collection of essays by the Institute of Economic Development of the Faculty of Economics at İstanbul University, whose *Problems of Turkey's Economic Development* (İstanbul: Sermet Matbaasi, 1972) covers planning, monetary policy, sectoral analysis, social problems, and Turkey's relations with the Common Market. Ş. İlkin and E. İnanç, eds., *Planning in Turkey*, publication no. 9 (Ankara: Middle East Technical University, 1967), zeroes in on Turkey's efforts to stimulate development. Maxwell J. Fry, in *Finance and Development Planning in Turkey* (Leiden: E. J. Brill, 1972), focuses on one of Turkey's most central and most intractable problems. A provocative work written by Suzanne Paine on the basis of early data, *Exporting Workers: The Turkish Case* (London: Cambridge University Press, 1974), questions the benefits to the sending country from the export of labor. Of a more general nature, Edwin J. Cohn's *Turkish Economic, Social, and Political Change* (New York: Praeger Publishers, 1970) attempts to integrate economic and political dimensions of change in Turkey. Bertil Walstedt, in *State Manufacturing Enterprise in a Mixed Economy: The Turkish Case* (Baltimore: Johns Hopkins University Press, for the World Bank, 1980), analyzes Turkey's industrial problems and, with a heavy emphasis on state economic enterprises, criticizes the capital-intensive, import-substitution approach. William Hale's *The Political and Economic Development of Modern Turkey* (London: Croom Helm, 1981) is, despite the title, a work concentrating almost exclusively on the economy of the Second Republic.

For an understanding of the present economic situation, the reader is referred to the series of OECD surveys on Turkey, which provides indispensable material; in particular, see *Turkey* (Paris: Organization for Economic Cooperation and Development, 1984 and previous years). For the point of view of the Turkish business community on the 1980 stabilization program, consult Turkish Industrialists and Businessmen's Association (TUSIAD), *The Turkish Economy: 1982* (İstanbul: Nurtan Matbaası, 1982); and the Union of Chambers of Commerce, Industry, Maritime Commerce and Commodity Exchanges of Turkey, *Economic Report* (Ankara: Ongun Kardeşler Matbaacılık Sanayii, 1982). The left-of-center assessment of the economic course that led up to the stabilization program animates Mehmet N. Uca's *Workers' Participation and Self-Management in Turkey: An Evaluation of Attempts and Experiences* (The Hague: Institute of Social Studies, 1983), and Berch Berberoglu's *Turkey in Crisis: From State Capitalism to Neo-Colonialism* (Westport, Conn.: Lawrence Hill, 1982). The notion that growing inequities in income distribution in Turkey may be incompatible with participatory democracy is found in Ergün Özbüdün and Aydın Ulusan, eds., *The Political Economy of Income Distribution in Turkey* (New York: Holmes & Meier, 1980).

CHAPTER 4: THE CONSTITUTION AND THE POLITICAL ORDER

For the basic documents of the Third Republic, see İlnur Çevik, ed., *Turkey 1983 Almanac* (Ankara: Turkish Daily News,

1983), which provides a rough summary of critical political party legislation as well as an English version of the 1982 constitution. The Turkish Directorate General of Press and Information of the Prime Ministry in its *Turkey: Yearbook 1983* (Ankara: Dönmez Ofset Basımevi, 1983) also contains the English translation of the constitution as well as considerable other recent economic and social data. For the provincial results of the constitutional referendum, see the *1983 Statistical Yearbook of Turkey* published by the Prime Ministry State Institute of Statistics. Thus far, the only full record of the November 1983 elections results by province can be found in the Turkish Official Gazette; in particular, see *Resmi Gazete* (November 14, 1983), pp. 13–59. Results of the vote for the major party candidates by province are also given in *Briefing* (Ankara) (November 21, 1983), pp. 13–15. For an unofficial tally of the March 1984 municipal elections on a nationwide basis, see Foreign Broadcast Information Service, vol. 7—Western Europe: Turkey, p. T6 (April 2, 1984). For a discussion of electoral engineering in the Second Republic, see Sabri Sayari, "Aspects of Party Organization in Turkey," *Middle East Journal* 30, no. 2 (Spring 1976):187–199.

CHAPTER 5: POLITICAL DYNAMICS

Trends in Turkish leadership patterns are analyzed in detail in Frederick W. Frey, *The Turkish Political Elite* (Cambridge, Mass.: MIT Press, 1965). For biographies of current leaders, see İlnur Çevik, ed., *Turkey 1983 Almanac* (Ankara: Turkish Daily News, 1983). Ergün Özbüdün, in his *Social Change and Political Participation in Turkey* (Princeton, N.J.: Princeton University Press, 1976), relates Turkey's experience in mobilizing voters to political theory. A more persuasive discussion of this relationship can be found in William M. Hale, ed., *Aspects of Modern Turkey* (London: Bowker, 1976), a stimulating collection of conference papers that also seeks to relate cultural differences and politics. George S. Harris's "Republic of Turkey" chapter in David E. Long and Bernard Reich, eds., *The Government and Politics of the Middle East and North Africa* (Boulder, Colo.: Westview Press, 1980), analyzes party trends. The rise of Islamic politics is treated in Şerif Mardin, "Religion in Modern Turkey," *International Social Science Journal*, no. 2 (1977):279–297. George S. Harris evaluates the role of religion in "Islam and the State in Modern Turkey," *Middle East Reveiw* 11, no. 4 (Summer 1979):21–26, 31. Light is shed on the rise of new elements in the middle class in Turkey in Leslie L. Roos, Jr., and Noralou P. Roos, *Managers of Modernization: Organizations and Elites in Turkey (1950–1969)* (Cambridge, Mass.: Harvard University Press, 1971). The notion that Turkey might be going through a basic political re-alignment with labor shifting to back the Republican Peoples party is put forth by Ergün Özbüdün and Frank Tachau, "Social Change and Electoral Behavior in Turkey: Toward a 'Critical Realignment'?" *International Journal of Middle East Studies* 6, no. 4 (October 1975):460–480. Joseph S. Szyliowicz investigates the background of the major disruptive factor in political life in the 1960s and 1970s—the emergence of youthful terrorists—in *A Political Analysis of Student Activism: The Turkish Case* (Beverly Hills, Calif.: Sage, 1972.) Two studies stress the foreign hand in promoting Turkish terror: the testimony of Aydın Yalçın on June 25, 1981, before the U.S. Senate, Committee on the Judiciary, Subcommittee on Security and Terrorism, *Terrorism, the Turkish Experience* (Washington, D.C.: Government Printing Office, 1981); and Paul B. Henze, *The Plot to Kill the Pope* (New York: Charles Scribner's Sons, 1983). Additional statistics on the characteristics of Turkish terrorists can be found in the report of a symposium held at Ankara University in April 1984: see *International Terrorism and the Drug Connection* (Ankara: Ankara University Press, 1984). For a preliminary analysis of the typology of political violence in Turkey in the late 1970s, see George S. Harris, "The Left in Turkey," *Problems of Communism* 29, no. 4 (July-August 1980):26–41.

CHAPTER 6: THE ROLE OF THE MILITARY

Military developments have proven difficult for outsiders to penetrate; hence the literature on this important subject is relatively limited. Dankwart A. Rustow, in "The Army and the Founding of the Turkish Republic," *World Politics* (July 1959):513–552, lays the basis for understanding the key role of the military, although given his unawareness of the plotting going on even then, he was sanguine about military subordination to the civilians. George S. Harris, in "The Role of the Military in Turkish Politics," *Middle East Journal* (Winter–Spring 1965):54–66, 169–176, has profited from his vantage point following the 1960 military intervention in investigating the continuing part played by officers in the political process. Ergün Özbüdün contributes to the same topic of analysis in his *The Role of the Military in Recent Turkish Politics* (Cambridge, Mass.: Harvard

University, Center for International Affairs, 1966). Kemal H. Karpat, in "The Military and Politics in Turkey, 1960–64: A Socio-Cultural Analysis of a Revolution," *American Historical Review* 75, no. 6 (October 1970):1654–1683, focuses on the same general period. Kenneth Fidel, in "Military Organization and Conspiracy in Turkey," *Studies in Comparative International Development*, no. 2 (1970–1971):19–43, inspects the narrower issue of plotting in the armed forces. The 1971 incomplete intrusion of the military into the Turkish political arena was not given prominence in studies of Turkey. Although he misses certain subtleties and complexities, Roger P. Nye, in "Civil-Military Confrontation in Turkey: The 1973 Presidential Election," *International Journal of Middle East Studies* (April 1977):209–228, calls attention to the key contest over electing Gürsel's successor. Kemal H. Karpat provides a preliminary analysis of the 1980 military takeover in his "Turkish Democracy at Impasse: Ideology, Party Politics and the Third Military Intervention," *International Journal of Turkish Studies* 2, no. 1 (Spring-Summer 1981):1–43.

CHAPTER 7: TURKEY IN THE WORLD

Turkish foreign policy has become a topic of serious study only within the past two decades. Salâhi R. Sonyel, in *Turkish Diplomacy 1918–1923: Mustafa Kemal and the Turkish Nationalist Movement* (Beverly Hills, Calif.: Sage, c. 1975), explains the critical years of the establishment of the Turkish state. Edward Weisband concludes that Turkey's policy of neutrality was the sole appropriate course open to it in World War II in his *Turkish Foreign Policy, 1943–1945* (Princeton, N.J.: Princeton University Press, 1973). Ferenc A. Vali, in *Bridge Across the Bosporous: The Foreign Policy of Turkey* (Baltimore: Johns Hopkins Press, 1971), considers decisionmaking as well as Turkey's foreign relations from all azimuths. George S. Harris, in *Troubled Alliance: Turkish-American Problems in Historical Perspective, 1945–1971* (Washington, D.C.: American Enterprise Institute, 1972), exposes the dynamics of Turkey's major alliance. Kemal H. Karpat and his contributors, in *Turkey's Foreign Policy in Transition 1950–1974* (Leiden: E. J. Brill, 1975), catalogue the broadening of Turkey's foreign relations structure. A Congressional Research Service report by Ellen Laipson and Richard F. Grimmett lays out U.S. interests in Turkey and analyzes changing trends in Turkey's foreign policy, with special emphasis on Cyprus and

Aegean issues: see U.S. House of Representatives, 96th Congress, 2nd session, Committee on Foreign Affairs, *Turkey's Problems and Prospects: Implications for U.S. Interests* (Washington, D.C.: Government Printing Office, 1980). Paul B. Henze, in *Turkey, the Alliance and the Middle East: Problems and Opportunities in Historical Perspective*, Working Paper no. 36 (Washington, D.C.: Wilson Center, 1982), carries the story closer to date. For more strictly military-related coverage, see Duygu B. Sezer's *Turkey's Security Policies*, Adelphi Paper no. 164 (London: International Institute of Strategic Studies (IISS), 1981). A Turkish Cypriot view of the most disruptive aspect of Turkey's international structure is provided by Rauf Denktash in *The Cyprus Triangle* (Winchester, Mass.: Allen & Unwin, 1982). Nuri Eren, in *Turkey, NATO, and Cyprus: A Deteriorating Relationship* (Paris: Atlantic Institute for International Affairs, c. 1977), gives the Turkish view of the troubles. Albert Wohlstetter, in "The Strategic Importance of Turkey and the Arms Embargo," *Journal of International Relations*, no. 3 (Summer 1978):101–109, details some of the consequences of U.S. retaliation over the Cyprus issue. Andrew Mango, in *Turkey: A Delicately Poised Ally*, Washington Paper no. 28 (Beverly Hills, Calif.: Sage, 1976), also treats this aspect of Turkey's relations. For a discussion of one contentious problem that has receded in saliency in Turkish-American relations, see James W. Spain, "The United States, Turkey and the Poppy," *Middle East Journal* 29, no. 3 (Summer 1975):295–309. James W. Spain's *American Diplomacy in Turkey: Memoirs of an Ambassador Extraordinary & Plenipotentiary* (New York: Praeger, 1984) provides a personal picture of U.S. diplomatic relations with Turkey in the 1980s.

*   *   *

Those who wish further guidance may consult the bibliography in Stanford J. Shaw's *History of the Ottoman Empire and Modern Turkey* (cited earlier). For more specialized subjects the reader is referred to Abraham Bodurgil, who, as the compiler of *Kemal Ataturk: A Centennial Bibliography (1881–1981)* (Washington, D.C.: Library of Congress, Government Printing Office, 1984), surveys articles as well as books and monographs. Somewhat more focused is Metin Tamkoç's *A Bibliography on the Foreign Relations of the Republic of Turkey, 1919–1967, and Brief Biographies of Turkish States-*

men, publication no. 11 (Ankara: Middle East Technical University, Faculty of Administrative Sciences, 1968). For continuing contemporary coverage, the bibliographical references in the *Middle East Journal* provide an extensive review of recent literature, both books and periodicals.

Index

Note: Diacritical marks are ignored for purposes of alphabetization in this index. Thus, for example, *Çakmak* precedes *Caliphate* instead of following it as in normal Turkish practice. Ottoman figures, having no true last names, are listed under their *first* given name.